ANTHOLOGY OF SCORES TO

A HISTORY

OF  IN

WESTERN CULTURE

Volume I: Antiquity through the Baroque Era

MARK EVAN BONDS

Department of Music

University of North Carolina at Chapel Hill

PEARSON

Prentice
Hall

Upper Saddle River, New Jersey 07458

Library of Congress Cataloging-in-Publication Data
Bonds, Mark Evan.
A history of music in Western culture / Mark Evan Bonds.
     p. cm.
   Includes bibliographical references and index.
   ISBN 0-13-014320-0
   1. Music—History and criticism. I. Title.
  ML160.B75 2003
780′.9—dc21

2002042493

President, Humanities/Social Sciences: Yolanda de Rooy
Vice President/Editorial Director: Charlyce Jones Owen
Senior Acquisitions Editor: Christopher T. Johnson
Editorial Assistant: Evette Dickerson
AVP, Director of Production and Manufacturing: Barbara Kittle
Development Editor: David Chodoff

Production Editor: Joseph Scordato
Cover Design: Laura Gardner
Manufacturing Manager: Nick Sklitsis
Manufacturing Buyer: Ben Smith
Music Permissioner: Elsa Peterson Ltd.
Marketing Manager: Chris Ruel
Marketing Assistant: Kimberly Daum
Cover Art: John Singer Sargent (1856–1925), American, Rehearsal of the Pasdeloup Orchestra, oil on canvas, SuperStock

This book was set by A-R Editions, Inc. and was printed and bound by The Courier Companies. The cover was printed by Coral Graphics.

© 2003 by Pearson Education, Inc.
Upper Saddle River, New Jersey 07458

Printed in the United States of America
10 9 8 7 6 5 4 3 2 1

Main textbook: 0-13-014320-0
Anthology of Scores Vol. 1: 0-13-014357-X
Anthology of Scores Vol. 2: 0-13-014359-6

PEARSON EDUCATION LTD.
PEARSON EDUCATION AUSTRALIA Pty. Ltd.
PEARSON EDUCATION SINGAPORE, Pte. Ltd.
PEARSON EDUCATION NORTH ASIA Ltd.
PEARSON EDUCATION CANADA, Ltd.
PEARSON EDUCACIÓN DE MEXICO, S.A. de C.V.
PEARSON EDUCATION–Tokyo, Japan
PEARSON EDUCATION MALAYSIA, Pte. Ltd.
PEARSON EDUCATION Upper Saddle River, New Jersey

CONTENTS

1. Epitaph of Seikolos (1st century C.E.)

a) Greek Notation

b) Modern Transcription

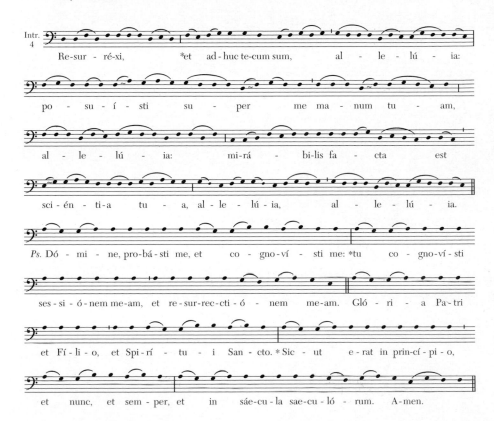

As long as you live, be happy;
do not grieve at all.
Life's span is short;
time exacts the final reckoning.

2. Plainchant **Mass for Easter Sunday**
a) Introit

Resurrexi, et adhuc tecum sum, alleluia:
posuisti super me manum tuam, alleluia:
mirabilis facta est scientia tua,
alleluia, alleluia.

Domine, probasti me, et cognovisti me:
tu cognovisti sessionem meam,
et resurrecctionem meam.

Gloria Patri et Filio,
et Spiritui Sancto.
Sicut erat in principio,
et nunc, et semper,
et in saecula saeculorum.   Amen.

I arose and am still with thee, alleluia:
thou hast laid thy hand upon me, alleluia;
thy knowledge is become wonderful,
alleluia, alleluia.

Lord, thou hast proved me, and known me:
thou hast known my sitting down
and my rising up.

Glory be to the Father, and to the Son,
and to the Holy Ghost.
As it was in the beginning,
is now, and ever shall be,
world without end.   Amen.

b) Kyrie

Ky - ri-e * e - le-i-son.*iij.* Chri - ste e - le-i-son.*iij.*

Ky - ri-e e - le - i-son.*ij.* Ky-ri - e *e - le - i-son.

Kyrie eleison.	Lord have mercy.
Christe eleison.	Christ have mercy.
Kyrie eleison.	Lord have mercy.

c) Gloria

Glo-ri - a in ex - cel-sis De-o. Et in ter - ra pax ho-mi-ni-bus bo-nae vo-lun-ta - tis.

Lau-da-mus te. Be-ne - di-ci - mus te. Ad-o-ra - mus te. Glo-ri-fi-ca - mus te.

Gra-ti - as a - gi-mus ti - bi pro-pter ma-gnam glo - ri - am tu-am.

Do - mi-ne De-us, Rex cae - le-stis. De - us Pa - ter o - mni-po - tens.

Do-mi - ne Fi-li u-ni - ge-ni-te Je - su Chri-ste. Do - mi-ne De-us, A - gnus De - i,

Fi - li - us Pa-tris. Qui tol - lis pec - ca-ta mun-di, mi-se - re-re no - bis.

Qui tol - lis pec - ca - ta mun-di, sus-ci - pe de-pre-ca - ti - o-nem no-stram.

Qui se - des ad dex - te-ram Pa-tris, mi-se - re-re no - bis. Quo-ni - am tu so-lus san-ctus.

Tu so-lus Do - mi - nus. Tu so - lus Al - tis - si-mus, Je - su Chri-ste.

Cum San-cto Spi-ri - tu, in Glo-ri-a De - i Pa - tris. A - men.

Gloria in excelsis Deo.	Glory to God in the highest.
Et in terra pax hominibus bonae voluntatis.	And on earth peace to men of good will.
Laudamus te. Benedicimus te.	We praise thee, we bless thee,
Adoramus te. Glorificamus te.	we adore thee, we glorify thee.
Gratias agimus tibi propter magnam gloriam tuam.	We give thee thanks for thy great glory.
Domine Deus, Rex caelestis.	O Lord God, King of heaven,
Deus Pater omnipotens.	God the Father almighty.
Domine Fili unigenite Jesu Christe.	O Lord, the only begotten Son, Jesus Christ.
Domine Deus, Agnus Dei, Filius Patris.	O Lord God, Lamb of God, Son of the Father.
Qui tollis peccata mundi,	Thou who takest away the sins of the world,
miserere nobis.	have mercy on us.
Qui tollis peccata mundi,	Thou who takest away the sins of the world,
suscipe deprecationem nostram.	receive our prayer.
Qui sedes ad dexteram Patris,	Thou who sittest at the right hand of the Father,
miserere nobis.	have mercy on us.
Quoniam tu solus sanctus.	For thou only art holy,
Tu solus Dominus.	thou only art Lord,
Tu solus Altissimus, Jesu Christe.	thou only art most high, O Jesus Christ,
Cum Sancto Spiritu,	with the Holy Ghost,
in Gloria Dei Patris. Amen.	in the glory of God the Father. Amen.

d) Collect

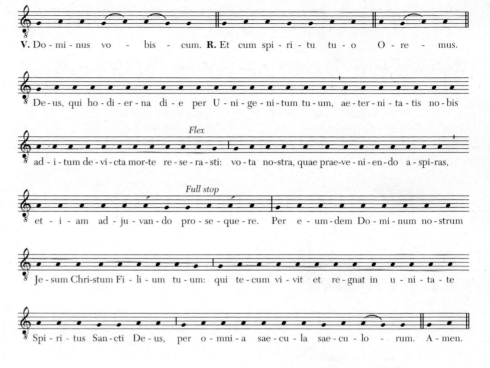

Dominus vobiscum.	The Lord be with you.
Et cum spiritu tuo. Oremus.	And with thy spirit. Let us pray.

Deus, qui hodierna die per Unigenitum tuum,	O God, who this day by thine only-begotten Son
aeternitatis nobis aditum devicta morte reserasti:	didst conquer death, opening unto us the gates
vota nostra, quae praeveniendo aspiras,	of everlasting life; to the desires of our hearts
etiam adjuvando prosequere.	which thou inspirest, do thou, by thy gracious help,
	enable us to attain.
Per eumdem Dominum nostrum	Through the same Jesus Christ,
Jesum Christum Filium tuum:	our Lord, thy Son,
qui tecum vivit et regnat	who with thee
in unitate Spiritus Sancti Deus,	in the unity of the Holy Ghost lives and reigns God,
per omnia saecula saeculorum. Amen.	world without end. Amen.

e) Epistle

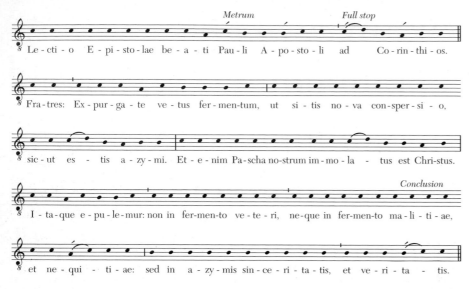

Lectio Epistolae beati Pauli Apostoli
ad Corinthios.
Fratres: Expurgate vetus fermentum,
ut sitis nova conspersio,
sicut estis azymi.
Etenim Pascha nostrum immolatus est Christus.
Itaque epulemur:
non in fermento veteri,
neque in fermento malitiae,
et nequitiae:
sed in azymis sinceritatis,
et veritatis.

Reading of the Epistle of St. Paul the Apostle
to the Corinthians.
Brethren, purge out the old leaven,
that you may be a new paste,
as you are unleavened;
for Christ our passover is sacrificed.
Therefore let us feast,
not with the old leaven,
nor with the leaven of malice
and wickedness,
but with the unleavened bread of sincerity
and truth.

f) Gradual

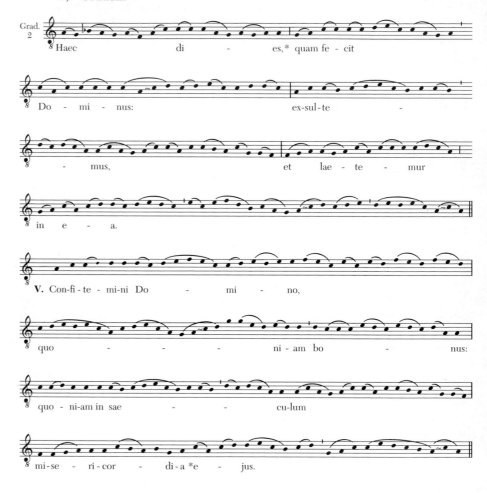

Haec dies, quam feci Dominus:
exsultemus, et laetemur in ea.

This is the day which the Lord hath made:
let us be glad and rejoice therein.

Confitemini Domino, quoniam bonus:
quoniam in saeculum misericordia ejus.

Give praise to the Lord, for he is good;
for his mercy endureth forever.

g) Alleluia

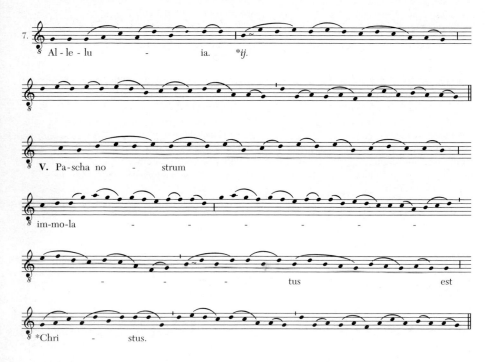

Al - le - lu - ia. *ij.

V. Pa-scha no - strum

im-mo-la - - - - - - - -

- - - tus est

*Chri - stus.

Alleluia.
Pascha nostrum immolatus est Christus.

Alleluia.
Christ our passover is sacrificed.

h) Sequence

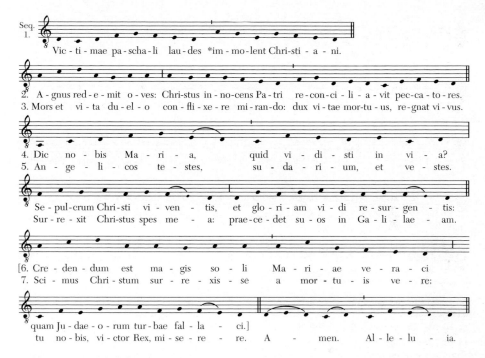

Seq. 1. Vic - ti - mae pa - scha-li lau - des *im - mo-lent Chri-sti - a - ni.

2. A - gnus red - e - mit o - ves: Chri-stus in - no-cens Pa - tri re - con - ci - li - a - vit pec-ca - to - res.
3. Mors et vi - ta du - el - o con - fli - xe - re mi - ran-do: dux vi - tae mor-tu - us, re - gnat vi - vus.

4. Dic no - bis Ma - ri - a, quid vi - di - sti in vi - a?
5. An - ge - li - cos te - stes, su - da - ri - um, et ve - stes.

Se - pul-crum Chri-sti vi - ven - tis, et glo - ri - am vi - di re - sur - gen - tis:
Sur - re - xit Chri-stus spes me - a: prae-ce - det su - os in Ga - li - lae - am.

[6. Cre - den - dum est ma - gis so - li Ma - ri - ae ve - ra - ci
7. Sci - mus Chri - stum sur - re - xis - se a mor-tu - is ve - re:

quam Ju - dae - o - rum tur - bae fal - la - ci.]
tu no - bis, vi - ctor Rex, mi - se - re - re. A - men. Al - le - lu - ia.

Victimae paschali	To the Paschal Victim let Christians
laudes immolent Christiani.	offer songs of praise.
Agnus redemit oves:	The Lamb has redeemed the sheep.
Christus innocens Patri reconciliavit peccatores.	Sinless Christ has reconciled sinners to the Father.
Mors et vita duelo conflixere mirando:	Death and life have engaged in miraculous combat.
dux vitae mortuus, regnat vivus.	The leader of life is slain, (yet) living he reigns.
Dic nobis Maria, quid vidisti in via?	Tell us, Mary, what you saw on the way?
Sepulcrum Christi viventis,	I saw the sepulchre of the living Christ
et gloriam vidi resurgentis:	and the glory of His rising;
Angelicos testes, sudarium, et vestes.	The angelic witnesses, the shroud and vesture.
Surrexit Christus spes mea:	Christ my hope is risen.
praecedet suos in Galilaeam.	He will go before his own into Galilee.
Credendum est magis soli Mariae	The truthful Mary alone is more to be believed
veraci quam Judaeorum turbae fallaci.	than the deceitful crowd of Jews.
Scimus Christum surrexisse a mortuis vere:	We know that Christ has truly risen from the dead.
tu nobis, victor Rex,	Thou conqueror and king,
miserere.	have mercy on us.
Amen. Alleluia.	Amen. Alleluia.

5

i) Gospel

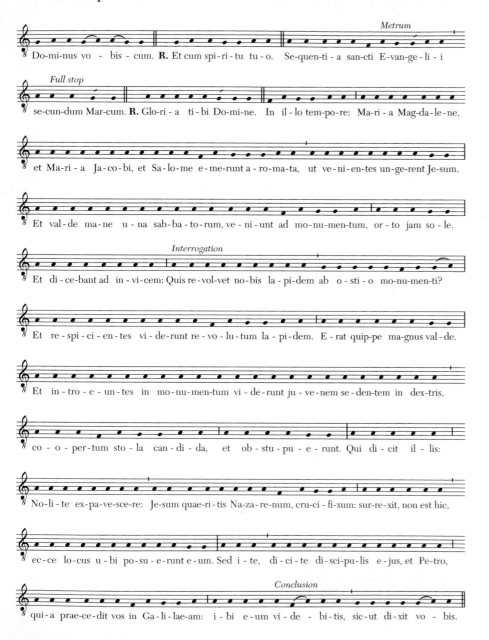

Dominus vobiscum.
Et cum spiritu tuo.
Sequentia sancti Evangelii
secundum Marcum.
Gloria tibi Domine.

In illo tempore:
Maria Magdalene, et Maria Jacobi,
et Salome emerunt aromata,
ut venientes ungerent Jesum.
Et valde mane una sabbatorum,
veniunt ad monumentum,
orto jam sole.
Et dicebant ad invicem:
Quis revolvet nobis lapidem
ab ostio monumenti?
Et respicientes viderunt revolutum lapidem.
Erat quippe magnus valde.
Et introeuntes in monumentum
viderunt juvenem sedentem in dextris,
coopertum stola candida,
et obstupuerunt.
Qui dicit illis:
Nolite expavescere:
Jesum quaeritis Nazarenum, crucifixum:
surrexit, non est hic,
ecce locus ubi posuerunt eum.
Sed ite, dicite discipulis ejus,
et Petro, quia praecedit vos in Galilaeam:
ibi eum videbitis, sicut dixit vobis.

The Lord be with you.
And with thy spirit.
Continuation with the holy Gospel
according to Mark.
Glory to thee, O Lord.

At that time,
Mary Magdalene, and Mary the mother of James,
and Salome bought spices,
that they might come and anoint Jesus.
And very early in the morning,
the first day of the week they came to the sepulchre,
the sun being then risen:
and they said one to another,
Who shall roll us away the stone from the door
of the sepulchre?
And looking, they saw the stone was rolled away:
for it was very great.
And entering the sepulchre,
they saw a young man sitting on the right side,
clothed in a white robe,
and they were astonished.
He said to them:
Be not affrighted;
you seek Jesus of Nazareth, who was crucified;
he is risen, he is not here;
behold the place where they laid him.
But go, tell his disciples,
and Peter, that he goeth before you into Galilee:
there you shall see him, as he told you.

j) Credo

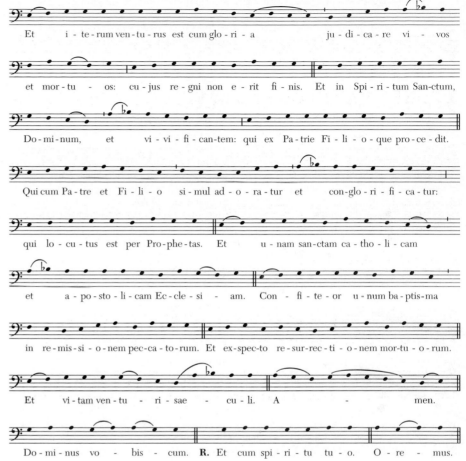

Credo in unum Deum.
Patrem omnipotentem,
factorem caeli et terrae,
visibilium omnium et invisibilium.
Et in unum Dominum Jesum Christum,
Filium Dei unigenitum.
Et ex Patre natum.
ante omnia saecula.
Deum de Deo, lumen de lumine,
Deum verum de Deo vero.
Genitum, non factum,
consubstantialem Patri:
per quem omnia facta sunt.

I believe in one God,
Father almighty,
maker of heaven and earth
and of all things visible and invisible.
And in one Lord Jesus Christ,
the only-begotten Son of God,
born of the Father
before all ages.
God of God, light of light,
true God of true God.
Begotten, not made,
being of one substance with the Father,
by whom all things were made.

Qui propter nos homines et propter nostram salutem descendit de caelis.	Who for us men and for our salvation came down from heaven.
Et incarnatus est de Spiritu Sancto ex Maria Virgine:	And was made incarnate by the Holy Ghost of the Virgin Mary,
Et homo factus est.	and was made man.
Crucifixus etiam pro nobis:	And was crucified for us
sub Pontio Pilato passus et sepultus est.	under Pontius Pilate. He suffered and was buried.
Et resurrexit tertia die,	And the third day he rose again
secundum Scripturas.	according to the Scriptures.
Et ascendit in caelum:	And ascended into heaven,
sedet ad dexteram Patris.	and sitteth on the right hand of the Father.
Et iterum venturus est cum gloria	And he shall come again with glory to judge
judicare vivos et mortuos:	the quick and the dead;
cujus regni non erit finis.	of whose kingdom there shall be no end.
Et in Spiritum Sanctum, Dominum,	And in the Holy Ghost,
et vivificantem:	Lord and giver of life,
qui ex Patrie Filioque procedit.	who proceedeth from the Father and the Son.
Qui cum Patre et Filio simul adoratur	Who, together with the Father and the Son,
et conglorificatur:	is worshiped and glorified;
qui locutus est per Prophetas.	who spake by the prophets.
Et unam sanctam catholicam	And one holy, Catholic,
et apostolicam Ecclesiam.	and Apostolic Church.
Confiteor unum baptisma	I acknowledge one baptism
in remissionem peccatorum.	for the remission of sins.
Et exspecto resurrectionem mortuorum.	And I look for the resurrection of the dead,
Et vitam venturi saeculi. Amen.	and the life of the world to come. Amen.
Dominus vobiscum.	The Lord be with you.
Et cum spiritu tuo.	And with thy spirit.
Oremus.	Let us pray.

k)   Offertory

Terra tremuit, et quievit,	The earth trembled and was still
dum resurgeret in judicio Deus,	when God arose in judgment,
alleluia.	alleluia.

1) Preface

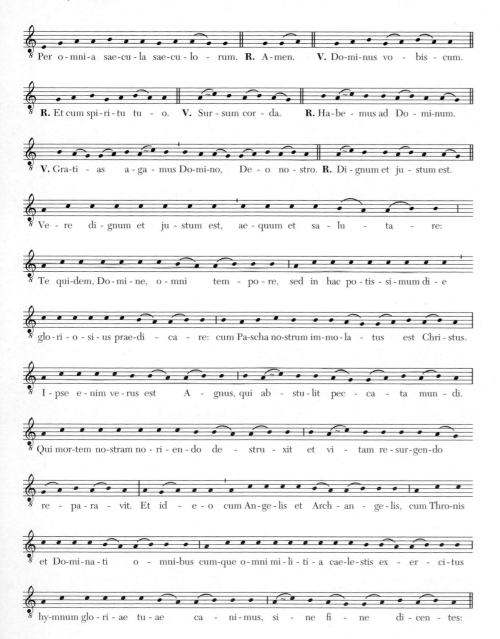

Per o-mni-a sae-cu-la sae-cu-lo-rum. **R.** A-men. **V.** Do-mi-nus vo-bis-cum.

R. Et cum spi-ri-tu tu-o. **V.** Sur-sum cor-da. **R.** Ha-be-mus ad Do-mi-num.

V. Gra-ti-as a-ga-mus Do-mi-no, De-o no-stro. **R.** Di-gnum et ju-stum est.

Ve-re di-gnum et ju-stum est, ae-quum et sa-lu-ta-re:

Te qui-dem, Do-mi-ne, o-mni tem-po-re, sed in hac po-tis-si-mum di-e

glo-ri-o-si-us prae-di-ca-re: cum Pa-scha no-strum im-mo-la-tus est Chri-stus.

I-pse e-nim ve-rus est A-gnus, qui ab-stu-lit pec-ca-ta mun-di.

Qui mor-tem no-stram no-ri-en-do de-stru-xit et vi-tam re-sur-gen-do

re-pa-ra-vit. Et id-e-o cum An-ge-lis et Arch-an-ge-lis, cum Thro-nis

et Do-mi-na-ti o-mni-bus cum-que o-mni mi-li-ti-a cae-le-stis ex-er-ci-tus

hy-mnum glo-ri-ae tu-ae ca-ni-mus, si-ne fi-ne di-cen-tes:

Per omnia saecula saeculorum.   Amen.
Dominus vobiscum.
Et cum spiritu tuo.
Sursum corda.
Habemus ad Dominum.
Gratias agamus Domino, Deo nostro.
Dignum et justum est.
Vere dignum et justum est,
aequum et salutare:
Te quidem, Domine, omni tempore,
sed in hac potissimum
die gloriosius praedicare:
cum Pascha nostrum immolatus est Christus.
Ipse enim verus est Agnus,
qui abstulit peccata mundi.
Qui mortem nostram noriendo
destruxit et vitam
resurgendo reparavit.
Et ideo cum Angelis et Archangelis,
cum Thronis et Dominati omnibus
cumque omni militia caelestis
exercitus hymnum gloriae tuae canimus,
sine fine dicentes:

World without end,   Amen.
The Lord be with you.
And with thy spirit.
Lift up your hearts.
We have lifted them up unto the Lord.
Let us give thanks to the Lord our God.
It is meet and just.
It is truly meet and just,
right and profitable to extol thee indeed
at all times, O Lord,
but chiefly with highest praise
to magnify thee on this day
when for us was sacrificed Christ our passover.
For he is the true Lamb
who has taken away the sins of the world;
who by dying himself
has destroyed our death;
and by rising again has bestowed a new life on us.
And therefore with the angels and archangels,
with the thrones and dominations,
and with all the array of the heavenly Host,
we sing a hymn to thy glory
and unceasingly repeat:

m) Sanctus

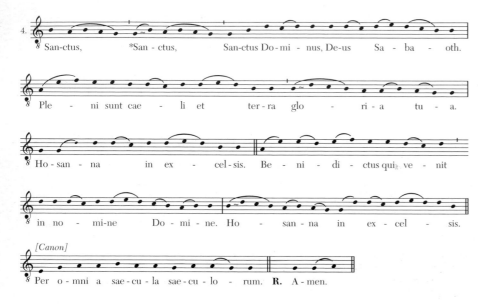

Sanctus, Sanctus, Sanctus
Dominus, Deus Sabaoth.
Pleni sunt caeli et terra gloria tua.
Hosanna in excelsis.
Benidictus qui venit in nomine Domine.
Hosanna in excelsis.
Per omni a saecula saeculorum. Amen.

Holy, holy, holy,
Lord God of Hosts.
The heavens and earth are full of thy glory.
Hosanna in the highest.
Blessed is he who comes in the name of the Lord.
Hosanna in the highest.
World without end. Amen.

n) Pater noster

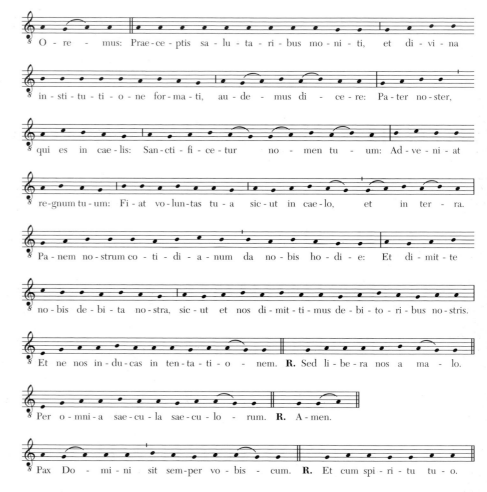

Oremus:
Praeceptis salutaribus moniti,
et divina institutione formati,
audemus dicere:
Pater noster, qui es in caelis:
Sanctificetur nomen tuum:
Adveniat regnum tuum:
Fiat voluntas tua sicut in caelo, et in terra.

Let us pray:
Thereto admonished by wholesome precepts,
and in words taught us by God himself,
we presume to say:
Our Father, who art in heaven;
hallowed by thy name:
thy kingdom come:
thy will be done on earth as it is in heaven.

Panem nostrum cotidianum da nobis hodie:
Et dimitte nobis debita nostra,
sicut et nos dimittimus debitoribus nostris.
Et ne nos inducas in tentationem.
Sed libera nos a malo.
Per omnia saecula saeculorum.   Amen.
Pax Domini sit semper vobiscum.
Et cum spiritu tuo.

Give us this day our daily bread;
and forgive us our trespasses
as we forgive those who trespass against us.
And lead us not into temptation.
But deliver us from evil.
World without end,   Amen.
The peace of the Lord be with you always.
And with thy spirit.

p) Communion

Pascha nostrum immolatus est Christus alleluia:
itaque epulemur in azymis
sinceritatis et veritatis,
alleluia, alleluia, alleluia.
Dominus vobiscum.   Et cum spiritu tuo.

Christ our passover is sacrificed, alleluia:
therefore let us feast with the unleavened bread
of sincerity and truth,
alleluia, alleluia, alleluia.
The Lord be with you.   And with thy spirit.

o) Agnus Dei

Agnus Dei,
qui tollis peccata mundi:
miserere nobis.
Agnus Dei,
qui tollis peccata mundi:
miserere nobis.
Agnus Dei,
qui tollis peccata mundi:
dona nobis pacem.

Lamb of God,
who takest away the sins of the world,
have mercy on us.
Lamb of God,
who takest away the sins of the world,
have mercy on us.
Lamb of God,
who takest away the sins of the world,
give us peace.

q) Post-Communion

O - re - mus. Spi - ri - tum no - bis Do - mi - ne, tu - ae ca - ri - ta - tis in - fun - de:

ut, quos sa - cra-men-tis pa - scha-li - bus sa - ti - a - sti, tu - a fa - ci - as pi - e - ta - te

con - cor - des. Per Do - mi - num no - strum Je - sum Chri-stum fi - li - um tu - um,

qui te - cum vi - vit et re - gnat in u - ni - ta - te e - jus-dem Spi - ri - tus

San - cti Fi - li - us. Per o - mni - a sae - cu - la sae - cu - lo - rum. **R.** A - men.

Do - mi - nus vo - bis - cum. **R.** Et cum spi - ri - tu tu - o.

r) Ite, missa est

8. I - te, mis - sa est, al - le - lu - ia, al - le - lu - ia.
R. De - o gra - ti - as, al - le - lu - ia, al - le - lu - ia.

Ite, missa est, alleluia, alleluia.
Deo gratias, alleluia, alleluia.

Go, the Mass has been said, alleluia, alleluia.
Thanks be to God, alleluia, alleluia.

Oremus.
Spiritum nobis Domine,
tuae caritatis infunde:
ut, quos sacramentis paschalibus satiasti,
tua facias pietate concordes.
Per Dominum nostrum
Jesum Christum filium tuum,
qui tecum vivit et regnat
in unitate ejusdem Spiritus Sancti Filius.
Per omnia saecula saeculorum. Amen.
Dominus vobiscum. Et cum spiritu tuo.

Let us pray.
Impart to our souls, O Lord,
the Spirit of thy love,
that those whom thou hast fed with this Paschal mystery
may be united in harmony by thy merciful goodness.
Through Jesus Christ,
our Lord, thy Son,
who with thee lives and reigns
in the same unity of the Holy Ghost.
World without end. Amen.
The Lord be with you. And with thy spirit.

3. Plainchant **Vespers on Easter Sunday**

a) Antiphon **Angelus autem Domini**

An - ge - lus au - tem Do - mi - ni *de - scen - dit de cae - lo,

et ac - ce - dens re - vol - vit la - pi - dem, et se - de - bat su - per e - um

al - le - lu - ia, al - le - lu - ia.

Angelus autem Domini descendit de caelo,
et accendens revolvit lapidem,
et sedebat super eum,
alleluia, alleluia, alleluia.

An angel of the Lord descended from heaven
and coming rolled back the stone
and sat upon it.

(Matt. 28:2)

b) Psalm 109 **Dixit Dominus**

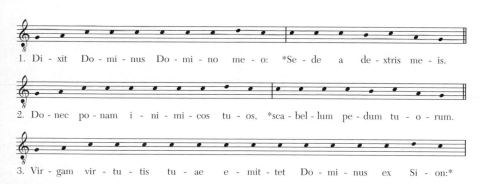
1. Di - xit Do - mi - nus Do - mi - no me - o: *Se - de a de - xtris me - is.

2. Do - nec po - nam i - ni - mi - cos tu - os, *sca - bel - lum pe - dum tu - o - rum.

3. Vir - gam vir - tu - tis tu - ae e - mit - tet Do - mi - nus ex Si - on:*

do - mi - na - re in me - di - o i - ni - mi - co - rum tu - o - rum.

4. Te - cum prin - ci - pi - um in di - e vir - tu - tis tu - ae in splen-do - ri - bus

san - cto - rum: *ex u - te - ro an - te lu - ci - fe - rum ge - nu - i te.

5. Ju - ra - vit Do - mi - nus, et non pae - ni - te - bit e - um: *Tu es sa - cer - dos

in ae - ter - num se - cun - dum or - di - nem Mel - chi - se - dech.

6. Do - mi - nus a de - xtris tu - is, *con - fre - git in di - e i - rae su - ae re - ges.

7. Ju - di - ca - bit in na - ti - o - ni - bus, im - ple - bit ru - i - nas:*

con - quas - sa - bit ca - pi - ta in ter - ra mul - to - rum.

8. De tor - ren - te in vi - a bi - bet: *pro - pte - re - a ex - al - ta - bit ca - put.

9. Glo - ri - a Pa - tri, et Fi - li - o, *et Spi - ri - tu - i San - cto.

10. Si - cut e - rat in prin - ci - pi - o, et nunc, et sem - per,*

et in sae - cu - la sae - cu - lo - rum. A - men.

1. Dixit Dominus Domino meo: Sede a dextris meis.	1. The Lord said to my Lord: Sit thou at my right hand.
2. Donec ponam inimicos tuos, scabellum pedum tuorum.	2. Until I make thy enemies thy footstool.
3. Virgam virtutis tuae emittet Dominus ex Sion: dominare in medio inimicorum tuorum.	3. The Lord will send forth the scepter of thy power out of Sion: rule thou in the midst of thine enemies.
4. Tecum principium in die virtutis tuae in splendoribus sanctorum: ex utero ante luciferum genui te.	4. With thee is the principality in the day of thy strength: in the brightness of the saints: from the womb before the day star I begot thee.
5. Juravit Dominus, et non paenitebit eum: Tu es sacerdos in aeternum secundum ordinem Melchisedech.	5. The Lord hath sworn, and he will not repent: Thou art a priest forever according to the order of Melchisedech.
6. Dominus a dextris tuis, confregit in die irae suae reges.	6. The Lord at thy right hand hath broken kings in the day of his wrath.
7. Judicabit in nationibus; implebit ruinas: conquassabit capita in terra multorum.	7. He shall judge among nations, he shall fill ruins: he shall crush the heads in the land of many.
8. De torrente in via bibet: propterea exaltabit caput.	8. He shall drink of the torrent in the way: therefore shall he lift up the head.
9. Gloria Patri, et Filio, et Spiritui Sancto.	9. Glory be to the Father, and to the Son, and to the Holy Spirit.
10. Sicut erat in principio, et nunc, et semper, Et in saecula saeculorum. Amen.	10. As it was in the beginning, is now, and ever shall be, world without end. Amen.

4. Plainchant Hymn **Pange lingua gloriosi corporis mysterium**

1. Pange lingua gloriosi Corporis mysterium, Sanguinisque pretiosi, Quem in mundi pretium Fructus ventris generosi Rex effudit gentium.	1. Sing, my tongue, the Savior's glory of His flesh the mystery sing; of the Blood, all price exceeding, shed by our immortal King, destined, for the world's redemption, from a noble womb to spring.
2. Nobis datus, nobis natus Ex intacta Virgine, Et in mundo conversatus, Sparso verbi semine, Sui moras incolatus Miro clausit ordine.	2. Of a pure and spotless Virgin born for us on earth below, He, as Man, with man conversing, stayed, the seeds of truth to sow; then He closed in solemn order wondrously His life of woe.
3. In supremae nocte coenae, Recumbens cum fratribus, Observata lege plene Cibis in legalibus, Cibum turbae duodenae Se dat suis manibus.	3. On the night of that Last Supper, seated with His chosen band, He the Pascal victim eating, first fulfills the Law's command; then as Food to His Apostles gives Himself with His own hand.

4. Verbum caro, panem verum
   Verbo carnem efficit:
   Fitque sanguis Christi merum,
   Et si sensus deficit,
   Ad firmandum cor sincerum
   Sola fides sufficit.

5. Tantum ergo Sacramentum
   Veneremur cernui:
   Et antiquum documentum
   Novo cedat ritui:
   Praestet fides supplementum
   Sensuum defectui.

6. Genitori, Genitoque
   Laus et jubilatio,
   Salus, honor, virtus quoque
   Sit et benedictio:
   Procedenti ab utroque
   Compar sit laudatio.
   Amen.

   (St. Thomas Aquinas, 1225–74)

4. Word-made-Flesh, the bread of nature
   by His word to Flesh He turns;
   wine into His Blood He changes;—
   what though sense no change discerns?
   Only be the heart in earnest,
   faith her lesson quickly learns.

5. Down in adoration falling,
   Lo! the sacred Host we hail;
   Lo! o'er ancient forms departing,
   newer rites of grace prevail;
   faith for all defects supplying,
   where the feeble senses fail.

6. To the everlasting Father,
   and the Son who reigns on high,
   with the Holy Ghost proceeding
   forth from Each eternally,
   be salvation, honor, blessing,
   might and endless majesty.
   Amen.

   [from *Liturgia Horarum*,
   trans. Fr. Edward Caswall (1814–78)]

5. Ordo virtutum

Hildegard von Bingen (1098–1179)

IV

[The Devil attempts to break into the circle of the Virtues to retrieve the Soul, but he is repulsed by them. It would be appropriate for them to repel the Devil by throwing flowers at him.
   Victory and Chastity will take up a chain and, with the help of one or more of the other Virtues, will bind the Devil, who will be left lying on the floor until the the end of the production.]

72. The Devil

Que es, aut unde venis?
Who are you, and from whence do you come?

Tu amplexata es me, et ego foras eduxi te.
You have embraced me, and I have led you forth.

Sed nunc in reversione tua confundis me;
But now in your turning back you confuse me;

Ego autem pugna mea deiciam te!
But I will hurl you down with my assault.

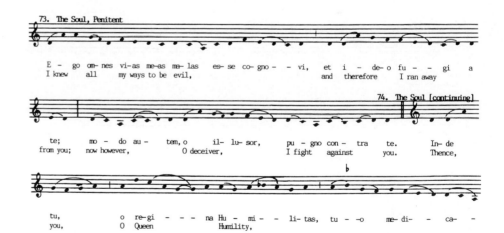

73. The Soul, Penitent

E - go om-nes vi-as me-as ma-las es-se co-gno - - vi, et i - de-o fu - - gi a
I knew all my ways to be evil, and therefore I ran away

74. The Soul [continuing]

te; mo - do au - tem, o il- lu-sor, pu - gno con - tra te. In - de
from you; now however, O deceiver, I fight against you. Thence,

tu, o re-gi - - - na Hu - mi - - li-tas, tu - -o me-di - - ca -
you, O Queen Humility,

15

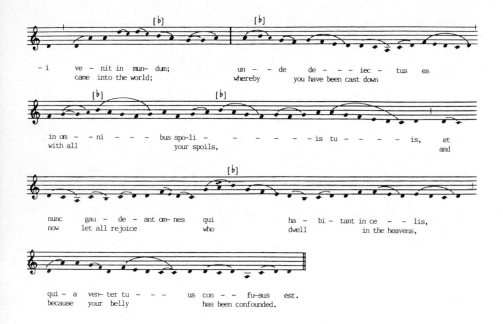

-i   ve - nit in mun- dum;   un - - de   de - - - iec - tus es
came into the world;   whereby   you have been cast down

in om - - ni - - - - bus spo-li - - - - - - is tu - - - - is,   et
with all   your spoils,   and

nunc   gau - de - ant om- nes   qui   ha - bi - tant in ce - - lis,
now   let all rejoice   who   dwell   in the heavens,

qui - a ven- ter tu - - - us con - - fu-sus est.
because   your belly   has been confounded.

6.   A chantar
Beatriz de Dia (d. ca. 1212)

W
204b

1   2   3   4   5   6   7   8   9   10

1. A   chan- tar m'es al   cor   que   non deu - ri - e

2. tant mi   ran- cun cele a   qui   sui   a - migs,

3. et   si   l'am mais que   nu - le   ren   qui   si - e;

4. non   mi   val ren bel- tat ni   cur - te - si - e

5. ne   ma   bon- taz ne   mon pres ne   mon sen;

6. al - tre- si   sui en - ga - nade et   tra - gi - de

7. qu'e - u - sse fait vers lui   de - sa - vi - nen- ce.

Text edition: Kussler-Ratyé, Béatrix, 164.   Music editions: Restori, Trovatori II, 244; Gérold, Moyen âge, 164, and Histoire, 274; Anglès, Canto popular, 422; Gennrich, Nachlass, #38.

The word "amigs" (2,9) as well as the word "cele" (2,5) suggests that the scribe assumed the speaker to be male, even though the rhyme, the meter, and the number of neumes demand the feminine form "amie" (also supported by the endings of the adjectives in verse 6).   7,7 The rhyme and meter of all other versions of this song demand the adjective "desavinen(t)", but the melody, which is identical to that of verses 2 and 4, demands a feminine ending.

A chantar m'es al cor que non deurie
tant mi rancun cele a qui sui amigs,

et si l'am mais que nule ren qui sie;
non mi val ren beltat ni curtesie
ne ma bontaz ne mon pres ne mon sen;
altresi sui enganade et tragide
qu'eusse fait vers lui desavinence.

To sing I must of what I'd rather not,
so much does he of whom I am the lover
    embitter me;
yet I love him more than anything in the world.
To no avail are my beauty or politeness,
my goodness, or my virtue and good sense.
For I have been cheated and betrayed,
as if I had been disagreeable to him.

7. **Cantigas de Santa Maria,** no. 140: **A Santa Maria dadas**

a

A San - ta   Ma - ri - a   da - das

b

se - jan   lo - o - res   on - rra - das.

c

1. Lo - e - mos   a sa   me - su - ra,
2. Lo - e - mos   a sa   no - bre - za,
3. Lo - e - mos   sa le - al - da - de,
4. Lo - e - mos   seu cou - si - men - to,
5. Lo - an - do - a,   que   nos   va - lla

d

seu prez   e sa   a - pos - tu - ra,
sa on - rra e   sa   al - te - za,
seu co - nort' e   sa   bon - da - de,
con - sell'   e cas - ti - ga - men - to,
lle ro - gue - mos   na   ba - ta - lla

e

e seu   sen   e   sa   cor du - ra,
sa mer - ce   e sa   fran - que - za,
seu a - corr'   e sa   ver - da - de,
seu ben,   seu   en - si - na - men - to
do mun - do   que   nos   tra - ba - lla,

f

mui máis   ca cen   mil ve - ga - das.
e sas   ver - tu - des pre - ça - das.
con lo - o - res   mui can - ta - das.
e sas   gra - ças   mui grã - a - das.
e do   dem' a   de - no - da - das.

A Santa Maria dadas	*To Holy Mary be*
sejan loores onrradas.	*given respectful praises.*

1. Loemos a sa mesura,
   seu prez e sa apostura,
   e seu sen e sa cordura,
   mui máis ca cen mil **vegadas.**
    A Santa Maria...

   Let us praise her dignity,
   her worth and her gracefulness,
   and her judgment and her wisdom,
   much more than a hundred thousand times.
    To Holy Mary,,,

(line 5)

2. Loemos a sa nobreza,
   sa onrra e sa alteza,
   sa mercee e sa franqueza,
   e sas **vertudes** preçadas.
    A Santa Maria...

   Let us praise her nobility,
   her honour and her rank,
   her mercy and her openness,
   and her treasured virtues.
    To Holy Mary...

(line 10)

3. Loemos sa lealdade,
   seu conort' e sa bondade,
   seu acorr' e sa verdade,
   con loores mui cantadas.
   A Santa Maria...

4. Loemos seu cousimento,
   consell' e castigamento,
   seu ben, seu ensinamento
   e sas graças mui grãadas.
   A Santa Maria...

5. Loando-a, que nos valla
   lle roguemos na batalla
   do mundo que nos traballa,
   e do dem' a denodadas.
   A Santa Maria...

Let us praise her loyalty,
her consolation and her bounty,
15 her help and her truth,
with praises ever sung.
   To Holy Mary...

Let us praise her attentiveness,
her counsel and admonition,
20 her goodness, her learning
and her graces so fine.
   To Holy Mary...

In praising her, let us ask her
that she be a strength to us in the battle
25 against this world, which causes us travail,
and against the devil, with valour.
   To Holy Mary...

8. Palästinalied

Walther von der Vogelweide (c. 1170–1230)

1. Nu alrest leb' ich mir werde,
   sît mîn sundic ouge ersiht.
   Lant daz hêre und ouch die erde,
   dem man vil der êren giht.

   Mir'st geschehn, des ich ie bat,
   ich bin komen an die stat,
   da got mennischlîchen trat.

1. Now for the first time I am alive,
   For my sinful eyes have beheld
   the land here and the very earth
   to which mankind gives such honor.

   I have that for which I so long prayed,
   I have come to the place
   where God walked as man.

9. Melismatic organum, **Kyrie Cunctipotens genitor deus** (Codex Calixtinus, ca. 1120–1130)

Cunctipotens genitor Deus, omni creator, eleyson.
Fons et origo boni pie luxque perennis, eleison.

Salvificet pietas tua nos bone rector, eleison.

Criste Dei forma virtus Patrisque sophia, eleyson.
Plasmatis humani factor lapsi reparator, eleison.

Ne tua damnetur jhesu factura benigne, eleison.

Amborum sacrum spiramen nexus amorque, eleyson.
Procedens fomes vitae fons purificans vis, eleison.

Purgator culpe venie largitor opimae, offensas dele sancto nos munere reple spiritus alme.

Omnipotent Father, God, creator of all, have mercy.
Fountain and origin of all good, holy and eternal light, have mercy.

May your holiness bring us salvation, O good Leader, have mercy.

Christ, appearance of God, power and wisdom of the Father, have mercy.
Maker of human flesh, savior of the fallen, have mercy.

Let not your creation be damned, O goodly Jesus.

Sacred breath of both, and combined love, have mercy.
Active former of life, fountain purifying us, have mercy.

Redeemer of sin, greatest dispenser of pardon, remove our misdeeds, fill us with holy reward, O nurturing Spirit.

(text and melody from additional source: Paris, Bibl. Nat. lat. 887, f.56, shown here in italics)

10. Organum **Haec dies**

Léonin (?) (fl. late 12th century)

21

R. Haec dies [quam fecit dominus: exsultemus
    et laetemur in ea.]
V. Confitemini Domino, quoniam bonus:
    quoniam in saeculum [misericordia eius].

R. This is the day [which the Lord hath made;
    let us rejoice and be glad in it.]
V. Give thanks unto the Lord; for he is good:
    for [his mercy endureth for ever].

(Ps. 118: 24, 29)
N.B. The text in brackets is performed in
plainchant, not organum, and therefore does
not appear in the original score.

11. Clausula **In saeculum**

in seculum   forever

12. Motet **Lonc tens ai mon cuer/In seculum**

1. *Lonc tens ai mon cuer assis*	1. I have fixed my heart on
2. *en bien amer.*	2. loving well for a long time.
3. N'onques vers amours ne fis	3. Never did I do anything to love
4. riens a blaumer;	4. which would incur blame.
5. ainz me sui mout entremis	5. Rather, I have made every effort
6. de lui loer.	6. to praise him.
7. Or ne puis mes endurer,	7. Now I can hold out no longer:
8. si m'a conquis;	8. he has conquered me;
9. de sa joie m'a si pris,	9. his joy has captured me so securely
10. n'i puis durer.	10. that I cannot go on.
11. Par mi sunt si pleur et si ris,	11. I am given to tears, then to laughter.
12. tout truis amer;	12. I find everything bitter;
13. quant le quit meillor trover,	13. when I think I will find love better,
14. lors me fet pis.	14. then he does something worse.
15. *Dieus quant je me doi*	15. God, when I should be
16. *la nuit reposer,*	16. resting at night,
17. *resveillent moi*	17. love's sweet pains
18. *li doz mal d'amer.*	18. waken me.

23

13. Motet **Huic main/ Hec dies**

1. *Hui main* au doz mois de mai,
2. desouz le solau levant,
3. en un vergier m'en entrai.
4. Desous un pin verdoiant
5. une pucele i trovai
6. roses coillant.
7. Lors me trai vers li;
8. de fine amour li pri.
9. Ele me respondi:
10. *"A moi n'atoucherés voz ja,*
11. *quar j'ai mignot ami!"*

1. This morning, in the sweet month of May,
2. just as the sun was rising,
3. I entered an orchard.
4. There under a lush green pine
5. I found a maiden
6. gathering roses.
7. Forthwith I approached her
8. and courteously declared my love for her.
9. She answered me:
10. "You will never touch me,
11. for I have a handsome sweetheart!"

14. Motet **A Paris / On parole / Frese nouvele**

a mes-tier, 10.pour so - la - cier 11.be-les da-mes a de-vis: 12.Et tout ce truev[e] on a Pa-ris.

en - tre-deus 8.de men - re feur pour ho - mes de - si - teus.

ve - le, mue-re fran - ce, mue-re, mue-re fran - ce!]

Triplum
1. On parole de batre et de vanner
2. et de foïr et de hanner;
3. mais ces deduis trop me desplaisent,
4. car il n'est si bone vie que d'estre a aise
5. de bon cler vin et de chapons
6. et d'estre aveuc bons compaignons,
7. liés et joiaus,
8. chantans, truffans et amorous,
9. et d'avoir, quant a mestier,
10. pour solacier
11. beles dames a devis:
12. Et tout ce truev[e] on a Paris.

Triplum
The talk is of threshing and winnowing,
of digging and ploughing.
Such pastimes are not at all to my liking.
For there is nothing like having one's fill
of good clear wine and capons,
and being with good friends,
hale and hearty,
singing, joking and in love,
and having all one needs
to give pleasure to beautiful women
to one's heart's content.
All of this is to be had in Paris.

Duplum
1. A Paris soir et matin
2. truev[e] on bon pain et bon cler vin,
3. bone char et bon poisson,
4. de toutes guises compaignons,
5. sens soutie, grant baudour,
6. biaus joiaus dames d'ounour;
7. et si truev[e] on bien entredeus
8. de menre feur pour homes desiteus.

Duplum
Morning and night in Paris
there is good bread to be found, good clear wine,
good meat and fish,
all manner of friends
of lively minds and high spirits,
fine jewels and noble ladies
and, in the meantime,
prices to suit a poor man's purse.

Tenor
1. Frese nouvele, muere france,
   muere, muere france!
2. Frese nouvele, muere france,
   muere, muere france!
3. Frese nouvele, muere france,
   muere, muere france!
4. Frese nouvele, muere france,
   muere, muere france!

Tenor
Fresh strawberries! Nice blackberries!
Blackberries, nice blackberries!
Fresh strawberries! Nice blackberries!
Blackberries, nice blackberries!
Fresh strawberries! Nice blackberries!
Blackberries, nice blackberries!
Fresh strawberries! Nice blackberries!
Blackberries, nice blackberries!

—Translated by Michael J. Freeman

15. Conductus **Flos ut rosa floruit**

I.

Flos ut ro - sa flo - ru - it, quan-do Vir - go ge - nu - it Ma - ri - a

Sal - va - to - rem om - ni - um, sum-mi Pa - tris Fi - li - um, no-va ge - ni - tu - ra.

II.

Qui di - vi - na gra - ci - a de - scen-dit ad in - fe - ra hu - ma - na,

Et sal - va - vit om - ni - a sum-ma cum po - ten - ci - a, no-va ge - ni - tu - ra.

I. Flos ut rosa floruit, quando Virgo genuit Maria
Salvatorem omnium, summi Patris Filium, *nova genitura.*

I. A flower bloomed like a rose, when the Virgin Mary gave birth
To the Savior of all people, the Son of the highest Father, *in a birth of utter newness.*

II. Qui divina gracia descendit ad infera humana,
Et salvavit omnia summa cum potencia, *nova genitura.*

II. In divine grace he came down to humanity below
And saved us all with his immense power, *in a birth of utter newness.*

III. Cantemus hymnum glorie, cantico leticie laudando,
Sollempnizantes hodie regi regum iusticie gracias agendo.

III. Let us sing a hymn of glory, praising him with a song of joy,
And celebrate today by giving thanks to the justice of the king of kings.

IV. Qui natus est de virgine mistico spiramine, *nova genitura.*
Ergo nostra concio psallat cum tripudio benedicat Domino.

IV. He was born of a virgin by a mystical spirit, *in a birth of utter newness.*
Therefore let this group dance and sing praises and bless the Lord.

26

16. Garrit Gallus / In nova fert / Neuma from Roman de Fauvel

Philippe de Vitry (?) (1291–1361)

48

ri - a. Rur - sus, ec - ce, Ja - cob fa - mi - li - a Pha - ra - o - ne al -

- a, Mox U - li - xis gau - dens fa - cun - di -

III

55

te - ro fu - ga - tur; Non ___ ut o - lim Iu - de

a, ___ Mox lu - pi - nis den - ti - bus ar - ma -

63

ve - sti - gi - a Sub - in - tra - re po - tens,

tus, ___ Sub Ter -

70

la - cri - ma - tur. In de - ser - to fa - me fla - gel - la -

si - tis mi - les mi - li - ci - a Rur - sus vi - vit in

76

tur. Ad - iu - to - ris ca - rens ar - ma - tu - ra,

vul - pem mu - ta - tus, ___

B. I

83

Quam - quam cla - mat, ta - men spo - li - a - tur;

Cau - da cu - ius, ___ lu - mi - ne pri - va - tus ___

91

Con - ti - nu - o for - san mo - ri - tu - ra. O

Le - o, ___ vul - pe im - pe - ran -

98

mi - se - rum ex - u - lum vox ___ du - ra! O Gal -

te, pa - ret. O - ves sug - git ___ pul - lis sa - ci - a -

II

28

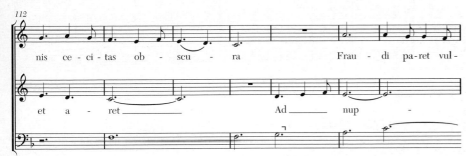

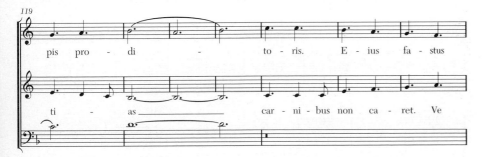

III

TRIPLUM

Garrit Gallus flendo dolorose	The cock babbles, lamenting sorrowfully,
Luget quippe Gallorum concio.	for the whole assembly of cocks°
Que satrape traditur dolose,	mourns because, while serving vigilantly,
Ex cubino sedens officio.	it is trickily betrayed by the satrap.
Atque vulpes, tamquam vispilio	And the fox,† like a grave robber,
in Belial vigens astucia	thriving with the astuteness of Belial,
De leonis consensu proprio	rules as a monarch with the consent
Monarchisat, atat angaria	of the lion himself.‡ Ah, what slavery!
Rursus, ecce. Jacob familia	Lo, once again Jacob's family
Pharaone altero fugatur;	is exiled by another Pharaoh.
Non ut olim lude vestigia	Not, as formerly, able to escape
Subintrare potens, lacrimatur.	to the homeland of Judah, they weep.
In deserto fame flagellatur.	Stricken by hunger in the desert,
Adiutoris carens armatura.	lacking the help of arms,
Quamquam clamat, tamen spoliatur,	although they cry out, they are robbed;
Continuo forsan moritura.	perhaps speedily they will die.

° Gallus: cock; or Gauls (the French)

† Enguerran de Marigny, chief councillor of the French king

‡ Philip IV the Fair

O miserum exulum vox dura!
O Gallorum garritus doloris,
Cum leonis cecitas obscura
Fraudi paret vulpis proditioris.
Eius fastus sustinens erroris
Insurgito: alias labitur
Et labetur quod haves honoris,
Quod mox in facinis tardis ultoribus itur.

O harsh voice of the wretched exiles;
O sorrowful babbling of the cocks,
since the dark blindness of the lion
submits to the fraud of the traitorous fox.
you who suffer the arrogance of his misdeeds,
rise up,
or what you have of honor is being or
will be lost, because if avengers are slow
men soon turn to evil doing.

DUPLUM

In nova fert animus mutatas
Dicere formas.
Draco nequam quam olim penitus
Mirabilis crucis potencia
Debellavit Michael inclitus,
Mox Absalon munitus gracia,
Mox Ulixis gaudens facundia,
Mox lupinis dentibus armatus,
Sub Tersitis miles milicia
Rursus vivit in vulpem mutatus,
Cauda cuius, lumine privatus
Leo, vulpe imperante, paret.
Oves suggit pullis saciatus.

Heu! suggere non cessat et aret
Ad nupcias carnibus non caret.
Ve pullis mox, ve ceco leoni!
Coram Christotandem ve draconi.

My heart is set upon speaking of forms
changed into new (bodies).§
The evil dragon that renowned Michael once
utterly defeated by the miraculous power
of the Cross,
now endowed with the grace of Absalom,
now with the cheerful eloquence of Ulysses,
now armed with wolfish teeth
a soldier in the service of Thersites,
lives again changed into a fox
whose tail the lion deprived
of sight obeys, while the fox reigns.
He sucks the blood of sheep and is satiated
with chickens.
Alas, he does not cease sucking and still thirsts;
he does not abstain from meats at the wedding feast.
Woe now to the chickens, woe to the blind lion.
In the presence of Christ, finally, woe to the dragon.
—RICHARD HOPPIN

§ Ovid *Metamorphoses,*1,1.

17. Messe de Nostre Dame: Kyrie
Guillaume de Machaut (ca. 1300–1377)

three times

31

18. Je puis trop bien ma dame comparer
Guillaume de Machaut

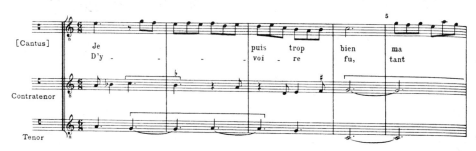

[Cantus]

Je _____ puis trop bien, ma
D'y _____ voi _____ re fu, tant

Contratenor

Tenor

e - ley - son.
e - ley - son.
e - ley - - - son.
e - - ley - - - son.

da - me com - pa - rer A l'y - ma - ge
belle et si sans per Que plus l'a - ma

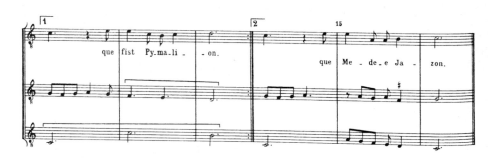

que fist Py-ma-li - - on.
que Me-de-e Ja - zon.

19. Douce dame jolie
Guillaume de Machaut

Douce dame jolie,	Fair sweet lady,
Pour Dieu ne pensés mie	for God's sake do not think
Que nulle ait signourie	that any woman has mastery
Seur moy, fors vous seulement.	over me, save you alone.

i   Qu'adès sans tricherie Chierie   For always without deceit / I have cherished you,

Vous ay, et humblement   and humbly
Tous les jours de ma vie Servie   served you / all the days of my life

Sans vilein pensement.   without any base thought.

Helas! et je mendie   Alas! I am bereft
D'esperance et d'aïe;   of hope and help;
Dont ma joie est fenie,   and so my joy is ended,
Se pité ne vous en prent.   unless you pity me.

Dous dame jolie . . .

ii   Mais vo douce maistrie   But your sweet mastery
   Maistrie   masters
Mon cuer si durement   my heart so harshly
Qu'elle le contralie   as to torment it
   Et lie   and bind it
En amours, tellement   with love, so much so

Qu'il n'a de riens envie   that it desires nothing
Fors d'estre en vo baillie;   but to be in your power;
Et se ne li ottrie   and yet your heart grants it
Vos cuers nul aligement.   no relief.

Douce dame jolie . . .

1. Je puis trop bien ma dame comparer
2. A l'image que fist Pymalion.
3. D'ivoire fu, tant belle et si sans per
4. Que plus l'ama que Medée Jazon.
5. Li folz toudis la prioit,
6. Mais l'image riens ne le respondoit.
7. Einse me fait celle qui mon cuer font,

8. *Qu'ades la pri et riens ne me respont.*

I can all too well compare my lady
To the image which Pygmalion made.
It was of ivory, so beautiful, without peer,
That he loved it more than Jason did Medea.
Out of his senses, he prayed to it unceasingly,
But the image answered him not.
Thus does she, who makes my heart melt, treat me,
For I implore her ever, and she answers me not.

33

iii   Et quant ma maladie
      Garie
  Ne sera nullement
  Sans vous, douce anemie,
      Qui lie
  Estes de mon tourment.

  A jointes mains deprie
  Vo cuer, puis qu'il m'oublie,
  Que temprement m'ocie,
Car trop langui longuement.

    Douce dame jolie . . .

And since my sickness
will not be cured
in any way
save by you, sweet enemy,
who are glad
at my distress,

then with hands clasped I pray
that your heart, since it neglects me,
may kill me soon,
for I have languished too long.

20.   Ma fin est mon commencement
Guillaume de Machaut

Ma fin est mon commencement
Et mon commencement ma fin.
Et teneure vraiement.
Ma fin est mon commencement.
Mes tiers chans trois fois seulement
Se retrogardę et einsi fin.
Ma fin est mon commencement
Et mon commencement ma fin.

My end is my beginning
and my beginning my end.
And holds indeed.
My end is my beginning.
My third one time only
is retrograde and ends thus.
My end is my beginning
and my beginning my end.

21. Tout par compas

Baude Cordier (fl. early 15th century)

Tout par compas suy composés
En ceste ronde proprement
Pour moy chanter plus seurement.

Regarde com suy disposés,
Compaing, je te pri chierement:

Tout par compas suy composés
En ceste ronde proprement

Trois temps entiers par toy posés
Chacer me pues joyeusement,
S'en chantant as vray sentement.

Tout par compas suy composés
En ronde proprement
Pour moy chanter plus seurement.

Seigneurs, je vous pri chierement,
Priés pour celi qui m'a fait.

Je dis a tous communement:

Seigneurs, je vous pri chierement,

Que Dieu a son definement
Li doint pardon de son meffait.

Seigneurs, je vous pri chierement
Priés pour celi qui m'a fait.

With a compass was I composed,
Properly, as befits a roundelee,
To sing me more correctly.

Just see how I am disposed,
Good friend, I pray you kindly:

With a compass was I composed,
Properly, as befits a roundelee,

Three times around my lines you posed,
You can chase me around with glee
If in singing you're true to me.

With a compass was I composed,
Properly, as befits a roundelee,
To sing me more correctly.

Good lords, I pray you kindly,
Pray for her who made me.

I say to all of you in common:

Good lords, I pray you kindly,

That God may, at her death,
Pardon her misdeeds.

Good lords, I pray you kindly,
Pray for her who made me.

22. Ecco la primavera

Francesco Landini (ca. 1325–1397)

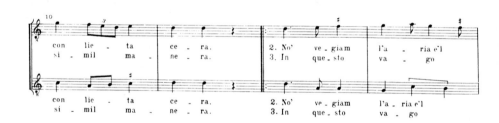

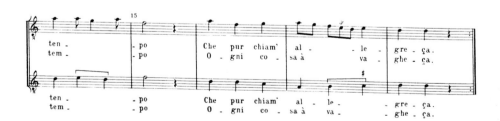

Ecco la primavera
che 'l cor fa rallegrare;
temp'è da 'nnamorare
e star con lieta cera.

No' vegiam l'aria e 'l tempo
che pur chiama allegreza;
in questo vago tempo
ogni cosa ha vagheza.

L'erbe con gran frescheza
e fiori copron prati
e gli alberi adornati
sono in simil maniera.

The time of Spring has come
which makes the heart rejoice;
it's time to fall in love
and to be of good cheer.

We see the air and weather
bringing about gladness;
in this lovely time
every thing has loveliness.

The meadows with fresh grass
and with flowers are covered;
and the trees are adorned
in a similar manner.

23. Non al suo amante
Jacopo da Bologna (fl. 1340–1360)

Non al suo amante più Diana piacque	[The goddess] Diana never pleased her lover more
Quando per tal ventura tutta nuda	when by chance he saw her quite naked
La vide in mezzo de le gelide acque.	among the chilly waters.
Ch'a me la pastorella alpestra e cruda,	That I [was pleased] by a rustic, curel shepherdess
Posta a bagnar un leggiadretto velo	intent on washing the graceful wispy veil
Ch'a l'aura il vago e biondo capel chiuda.	that protects her pretty blond hair from the breeze.
Tal che mi fece quando gli arde'l cielo,	So that although the sky burned hot
Tutto tremar d'un amoroso gielo.	my whole body trembled with the cold chill of love.
— Francesco Petrarca (1304—1374)	

24. A poste messe

Lorenzo da Firenze (d. 1372 or 1373)

41

A poste messe veltri et gran mastini
"Te, te Villan te, te Baril!" Chiamando,
"Ciof, ciof, quì quì, ciof

Bracchi e segugi per boschi aizzando,

"Ecco, ecco là, ecco là!"
"Guarda, guarda quà."
"Lassa, lassa, lassa."
"O tu, o tu, o tu."
"Passa passa passa."

La cerbia uscì al grido e al l'abbaio.
Bianca lattata col collar di vaio.

A ricolta bu, bu, bu, bu, bu
bu, bu, bu, bu, bu, sanza corno,
Tatim tatim tatim tatim tatim
titon titon titon tatim tatim
tatim tatim sonava per iscorno
No no no no no.

All in their places, greyhounds, mastiffs ready,
"Hey, hey, Villán," "Hey, Hey, Baríl" . . . And
   shout
"Ciof, ciof . . . here . . . here . . . ciof,"
Urging brachs and bloodhounds on the outing.

This way, that way . . . where?
Look, look, over there . . .
Slow! . . . slow! . . . slow!
Hey you . . . you . . . you . . .
Go! . . . go! . . . go! . . .

Midst shouts and barks, the doe emerged at bay,
Milky white, with neck of spotted gray.

To rally! Bu, bu, bu, bu, bu
Bu, bu, bu, bu, bu, without the horn,
Tatim, tatim, tatim, tatim, tatim,
Titon, titon, titon, tatim, tatim,
Tatim, tatim, it sounded as in scorn . . .
No, no, no, no, no!

25. Doctorum principem / Melodia suavissima / Vir mitis

Johannes Ciconia (ca. 1370–1412)

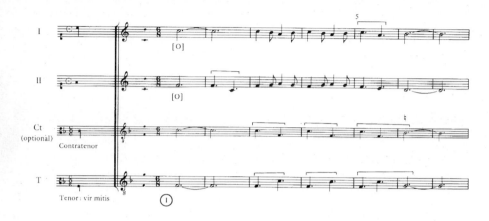

44

A: *Voice I:*

1. [O] Doctorum principem super ethera
   revocant virtutum digna merita.

   Ergo vive voci detur opera,

   promat mentis fervor, intus concita.

2. O Francisce Zabarelle, gloria,
   doctor, *honos* et lumen Patavorum,
   vive felix de tanta victoria;
   pro te virescit fama, P*at*avorum.

3. O Francisce Zabarelle, pabula
   parasti pastoribus armentorum,
   quibus pascant oves; grata secula

   te pro munete revocant laborum.

B: *Voice II:*

1. [O] Melodia suavissima cantemus,
   tangant voces melliflue sidera,
   concord*ie* carmen liram sonemus,
   resonet per choros pulsa cithara.

2. O Francisce Zabarelle, protector,
   imo verus pater rei publice,
   illos ad se vocat terum conditor,
   qui fortu*ne* miserentur lubrice.

3. O Francisce Zabarelle, causas
   specularis omnium creatorum;

   tu*as* posteri resonebunt musas
   per omnia secula seculorum.

1. The fitting merits of his deed
   extol the prince of teachers to beyond the
       skies.
   Therefore let sincerely summoned care be
       given to living voice,
   let fervour of mind show forth.

2. O Francesco Zabarella, glory,
   teacher, honour, light of Padua,
   live contented at such a triumph.
   Padua's fame will increase because of thee.

3. O Francesco Zabarella, thou hast provided
   nourishment for the shepherds of the flocks,
   on which they may graze their sheep. A
       grateful world
   proclaims thee as reward for thy labours.

1. Let us sing with sweetest melody,
   let our mellifluous voices reach the stars,
   let us sound the harmonious lyre,
   let the plucked cithara resound throughout
       the choirs.

2. O Francesco Zabarella, protector,
   yea, true father of the commonweal,
   the Maker calls unto himself
   those that have pity for fleeting misfortune.

3. O Francesco Zabarella,
   thou dost watch over the affairs of all
       creatures:
   posterity will resound thy praises
   for ever and ever.

26. Sumer is icumen in

Anonymous

46

47

MIDDLE ENGLISH:

Sumer is icumen in,
Lhude sing cuccu.
Groweth sed and bloweth med,
And springth the wde nu.
Sing cuccu.
Awe bleteth after lomb,
Lhouth after calve cu;
Bulluc sterteth,
bucke verteth.
Murie sing cuccu.
Cuccu, cuccu.
Wel singes thu cuccu.
Ne swik thu naver nu.

Summer has come in,
Loudly sing, cuckoo!
Grows the seed and blooms the meadow,
And the woods springs anew.
Sing, cuckoo!
The ewe bleats after her lamb,
The cow lows after her calf;
The bull jumps, the stag leaps,
Merrily sing, cuckoo!
Cuckoo, cuckoo,
Well sing you, cuckoo.
Nor stop now!
Sing cuckoo now, sing cuckoo!
Sing cuckoo now, sing cuckoo!

LATIN:

Perspice christicola: quae dignacio!
Caelicus agricola, pro vitis vicio,

Filio non parcens exposuit mortis exicio;

Qui captivos semivivos a supplicio
Vitae donat et secum coronat in coeli solio.
Resurrexit Dominus.

Behold, Christian, what dignity!
The celestial farmer [God], because of the
    weakness of life [the vine]
Did not spare his son, but exposed him to the
    fate of death;
He who gives life to those half-alive captives,
    delivers them from punishment,
and crowns them in the heavenly throne.
The Lord is risen.

PES:
Sing cuccu nu, Sing cuccu.

Sing cuccu, Sing cuccu nu.

Sing cuckoo now, Sing cuckoo.

Sing cuckoo, Sing cuckoo now.

27. Edi be thu, heven-queene

Anonymous

Baritone

Guitar[1]
(or other suitable
plucked string
instrument)

1. Edi be thu, heven-quee - ne, fol - kes froovre and en - gles blis,
2. Thu a - sti - ye so dai - rew - e de - leth from the der - ke night.
3. Sprung - e blostm of o - ne roo - te, th'o - li gost thee rest up - on;
4. Erth art tu to goo - de see - de, on thee ligh - te th'e - ven-dew;
5. Mo - der ful of thew - es heen - de, mai - de dreigh and wel i - taught,

maid un - wem - med, mo - der clee - ne, swich in world non o - ther nis.
Of thee sprong a lee - me new - e; al this world hit hath i - light.
that was for man - kin - nes boo - te and her soul a - lee - se for on.
of thee sprong thet e - di blee - de, th'o - li gost hit on thee sew.
ich am in thi lu - ve - been - de and to thee is al mi draught.

On thee hit is wel eth - seen of al - le wim - men thu hast the pris. Mi
Nis no maid of thi - ne hew - e, so fair, so schee - ne, so ru - di, so bright; mi
Lev - di mil - de, soft and swoot, ich cri - e mer - ci, ich am thi mon, to
Bring us ut of kar, of dree - de that E - ve bit - ter - lich us brew; thu
Thu me schild, ye from the feend, as thu art free and wilt and maught, and

swee - te lev - di, heer mi been and rew of me yif thi will is.
lev - di sweet, of me thu rew and ha - ve mer - ci of thi knight.
hon - de bo - then and to foot on al - le wi - se that ich kon.
schalt us in - to hev - ne lee - de, wel sweet is us thet il - ke dew.
help me to mi li - ves eend and ma - ke with thi su - ne saught.

[1] This part may also be sung.

[2] Small notes to be used only in vocal performance.

---

1. Edi be thu, heven-queene,
folkes froovre and engles blis,
maid unwemmed, moder cleene,
swich in world non other nis.
On thee hit is wel ethseen
of alle wimmen thu hast the pris.
Mi sweete levdi, heer mi been
and rew of me yif thi will is.

2. Thu astiye so dairewe
deleth from the derke night.
Of thee sprong a leeme newe;
al this world hit hath ilight.
Nis no maid of thine hewe,
so fair, so scheene, so rudi, so bright;
mi sweet levdi, of me thu rew
and have merci of thi knight.

3. Sprunge blostm of one roote,
th'oli gost thee rest upon;
that was for mankinnes boote
and her soul aleese for on.
Levdi milde, soft and swoot,
ich crie merci, ich am thi mon,
to honde bothen and to foot
on alle wise that ich kon.

4. Erth art tu to goode seede,
on thee lighte th'evendew;
of thee sprong thet edi bleede,
th'oli gost hit on thee sew.
Bring us ut of kar, of dreede
that Eve bitterlich us brew;
thu schalt us into hevne leede,
wel sweet is us thet ilke dew.

5. Moder ful of thewes heende,
maide dreigh and wel itaught,
ich am in thi luvebeende
and to thee is al mi draught.
Thu me schild,
ye from the feend,
as thu art free
and wilt and maught,
and help me to mi lives eend
and make with thi sune saught.

---

1. Blessed be thou, queen of heaven,
people's comfort and angel's bliss,
maid unblemished, mother pure,
such as no other is in the world.
In thee it is very evident
that of all women thou hast the highest place.
My sweet lady, hear my prayer
and show pity on me if it is thy will.

2. Thou didst rise up as dawn
divides from the dark night.
From thee sprang a new sunbeam;
it has lit all this world.
There is no maid of thy complexion—
so fair, so beautiful, so ruddy, so bright;
my lady sweet, on me show pity,
and have mercy on thy knight.

3. Blossom sprung from a single root,
the Holy Ghost rested upon thee;
that was for mankind's salvation,
and to free their souls in exchange for one.
Gentle lady, soft and sweet,
I beg forgiveness, I am thy man,
both hand and foot,
in every way that I can be.

4. Thou art soil for good seed,
on thee the heavenly dew alighted;
from thee sprang that blessed fruit—
the Holy Ghost sowed it in thee.
Bring us out of the misery and fear
that Eve bitterly brewed for us;
thou shalt lead us into heaven—
very sweet to us is that same dew.

5. Mother full of gracious virtues,
maiden patient and well-instructed,
I am in the bonds of thy love
and all my attraction is towards thee.
Shield thou me,
yes from the fiend,
as thou art generous
and art willing and able,
and help me to my life's end
and reconcile [me] with thy son.

28. La quinte estampie real

Anonymous

29. Quam pulchra es

John Dunstable (ca. 1390–1453)

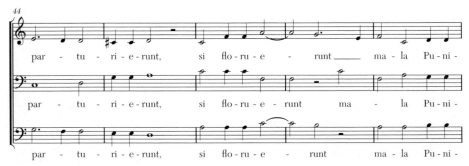

Quam pulchra es et quam decora,
  carissima in deliciis.
Statura tua assimilata est palme,
  et ubera tua botris.
Caput tuum ut Carmelus,
  collum tuum sicut turris eburnea.
Veni, dilecte mi,
egrediamur in agrum,
et videamus si flores fructus parturierunt,
  si floruerunt mala Punica.
Ibi dabo tibi ubera mea.
Alleluia.

—The Song of Solomon 7:6–12

How fair and pleasant you are,
  O loved one in delights.
You are stately as a plam tree,
  and your breasts are like its clusters.
Your head crowns you like Carmel:
  your neck is like an ivory tower.
Come, my beloved,
let us go forth into the fields,
and see whether the grape blossoms have opened
  and the pomegranates are in bloom
There I will give you my love.
Alleluia.

—Adapted from the Revised Standard Version
of the Bible

30. Flos florum

Guillaume Du Fay (ca. 1400–1474)

Flos florum,
Fons hortorum,
Regina polorum,

Spes veniae,
Lux laetitiae,
Medicina dolorum,

Virga recens
Et virgo decens,
Forma bonorum:

Parce reis
Et opem fer eis
In pace piorum,

Pasce tuos,
Succure tuis,
Miserere tuorum!

Flower of flowers,
Fount of gardens,
Queen of heaven,

Hope of pardon,
Light of joy,
Cure of pain,

Staff that guides,
Decorous maiden,
Model of goodness:

Spare the guilty
And bring them reward
Through the peace of the righteous,

Feed thine own,
Help thine own,
Have mercy upon thine own.

31. Conditor alme siderum

Guillaume Du Fay

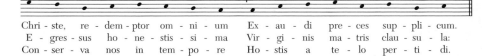

1. Con - di - tor al - me si - de - rum, Ae - ter - na lux cre - den - ti - um,
3. Ver - gen - te mun - di ve - spe - re U - ti spon - sus de tha - la - mo
5. Te de - pre - ca - mur a - gi - e Ven - tu - re iu - dex sae - cu - li

Chri - ste, re - dem - ptor om - ni - um Ex - au - di pre - ces sup - pli - cum.
E - gres - sus ho - ne - stis - si - ma Vir - gi - nis ma - tris clau - su - la:
Con - ser - va nos in tem - po - re Ho - stis a te - lo per - ti - di.

[Superius]

2. Qui __ con - do - lens in te - ri - tu Mor - tis per -
4. Cu - jus for - ti po - ten - ti - ae Ge - nu cur -
6. Laus, __ ho - nor, vir - tus, glo - ri - a De - o pa -

Bourdon

2. Qui __ con - do - lens in te - ri - tu Mor - tis per -
4. Cu - jus for - ti po - ten - ti - ae Ge - nu cur -
6. Laus, __ ho - nor, vir - tus, glo - ri - a De - o pa -

Tenor

Qui condolens

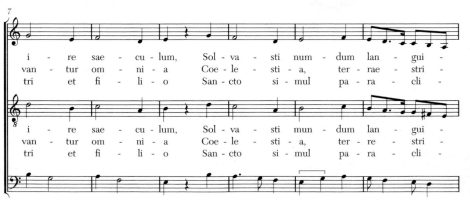

i - re sae - cu - lum, Sol - va - sti num - dum lan - gui -
van - tur om - ni - a Coe - le - sti - a, ter - rae - stri -
tri et fi - li - o San - cto si - mul pa - ra - cli -

i - re sae - cu - lum, Sol - va - sti num - dum lan - gui -
van - tur om - ni - a Coe - le - sti - a, ter - re - stri -
tri et fi - li - o San - cto si - mul pa - ra - cli -

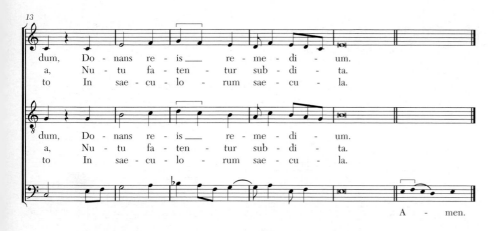

dum, Do - nans re - is _ re - me - di - um.
a, Nu - tu fa - ten - tur sub - di - ta.
to In sae - cu - lo - rum sae - cu - la.

dum, Do - nans re - is _ re - me - di - um.
a, Nu - tu fa - ten - tur sub - di - ta.
to In sae - cu - lo - rum sae - cu - la.

A - men.

Conditor alme siderum,	Creator of the stars of night,
Aeterna lux credentium,	Thy people's everlasting light,
Christe, redemptor omnium	Jesu, Redeemer, save us all,
Exaudi preces supplicum.	and hear Thy servants when they call.
Qui condolens in teritu	Thou, grieving that the ancient curse
Mortis perire saeculum,	should doom to death a universe,
Solvasti mundum languidum,	hast found the medicine, full of grace,
Donans reis remedium.	to save and heal a ruined race.
Vergente mundi vespere	Thou camest, the Bridegroom of the Bride,
Uti sponsus de thalamo	as drew the world to evening tide,
Egressus honestissima	proceeding from a virgin shrine,
Virginis matris clausula:	the spotless Victim all divine.
Cujus forti potentiae	At whose dread Name, majestic now,
Genu curvantur omnia	all knees must bend, all hearts must bow;
Coelestia, terraestria,	and things celestial Thee shall own,
Nutu fatentur subdita.	and things terrestrial Lord alone.
Te deprecamur agie	O Thou whose coming is with dread,
Venture iudex saeculi	to judge and doom the quick and dead,
Conserva nos in tempore	preserve us, while we dwell below,
Hostis a telo pertidi.	from every insult of the foe.
Laus, honor, virtus, gloria	To God the Father, God the Son,
Deo patri et filio	and God the Spirit, Three in One,
Sancto simul paraclito	laud, honor, might, and glory be,
In saeculorum saecula. Amen.	from age to age eternally. Amen.

32. Nuper rosarum flores

Guillaume Du Fay

[Triplum]

1. Nu - per ro - sa - rum flo - res

[Motetus]

1. Nu - per ro - sa - rum flo - res

Tenor 2

Terribilis est locus iste

Tenor 1

Terribilis est locus iste

Ex _ do - no pon - ti - fi - cis Hi - e - me li - cet _ hor - ri - da

Ex do - no pon - ti - fi - cis Hi - e - me _ li - cet hor - ri - da

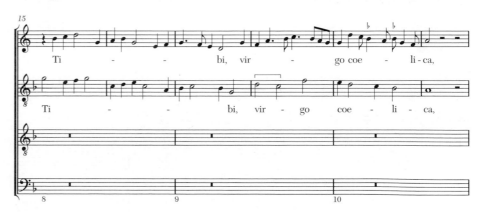

Ti - bi, vir - go coe - li - ca,

Ti - bi, vir - go coe - li - ca,

Hodie vicarius
Jesu Christi et Petri
Successor EUGENIUS
Hoc idem amplissimum
Sacris templum manibus
Sanctisque liquoribus
Consecrare dignatus est.

Igitur, alma parens,
Nati tui et filia,
Virgo decus virginum,
Tuus te FLORENTIAE
Devotus orat populus,
Ut qui mente et corpore
Mundo quicquam exoravit,

Oratione tua
Cruciatus et meritis
Tui secundum carnem
Nati domini sui
Grata beneficia
Veniamque reatum
Accipere mereatur.
Amen.

Today the Vicar
of Jesus Christ and Peter's
successor, Eugenius,
this same most spacious
sacred temple with his hands
and with holy waters
he is worthy to consecrate.

Therefore, gracious mother
and daughter of your offspring,
Virgin, ornament of virgins,
your, Florence's, people
devoutly pray
so that together with all mankind,
with mind and body, their
entreaties may move you.

Through your prayer,
your anguish and merits,
may [the people] deserve to
receive of the Lord,
born of you according to the flesh,
the benefits of grace
and the remission of sins.
Amen.

–Translation by William Bowen

Nuper rosarum flores
Ex dono pontificis
Hieme licet horrida,
Tibi, virgo coelica,
Pie et sancte deditum
Grandis templum machinae
Condecorarunt perpetim.

Recently roses [came]
as a gift of the Pope,
although in cruel winter,
to you, heavenly Virgin.
Dutifully and blessedly is dedicated
[to you] a temple of magnificent design.
May they together be perpetual ornaments.

33. Ave Maria . . . virgo serena

Josquin des Prez (c. 1450–1521)

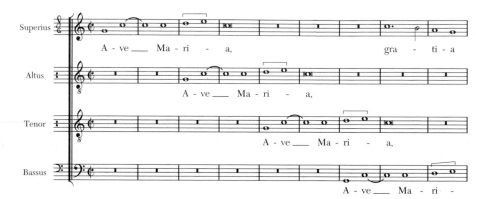

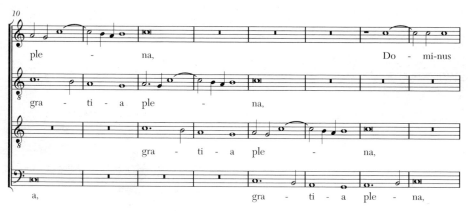

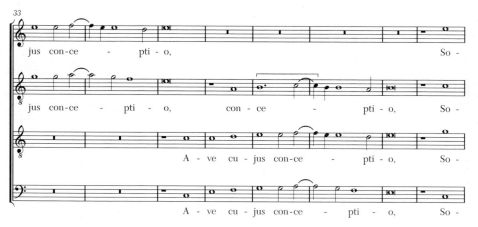

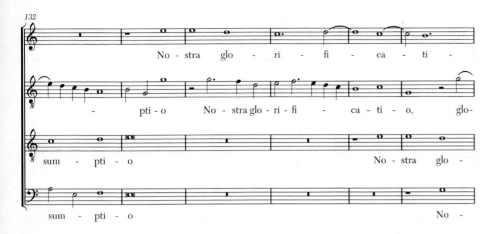

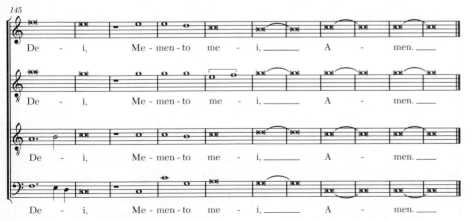

Ave Maria, gratia plena:	Hail Mary, full of grace:
Dominus tecum, Virgo serena	The Lord is with you, serene virgin.

Ave cuius conceptio,	Hail, whose conception,
solemni plena gaudio,	full of solemn joy,
Caelestia, terrestria,	fills the heavens and the earth
nova replet laetitia.	with new rejoicing.

Ave cuius nativitas,	Hail, whose birth
nostra fuit solemnitas,	was our festival,
Ut lucifer lux oriens,	As the light-bearing dawn
verum solem praeveniens.	heralds the true sunrise.

Ave pia humilitas,	Hail, blessed humility,
cuius annuciatio	whose annunciation
Nostra fuit salvatio.	Was our salvation.

Ave vera virginitas,	Hail, true virginity,
immaculata castitas,	immaculate chastity,
Cuius purificatio	whose purification
nostra fuit purgatio.	was our cleansing.

Ave praeclara omnibus,	Hail, foremost
angelicis virtutibus,	among all angelic virtues,
Cuius fuit assumptio,	Whose assumption was
nostra glorificatio.	our glorification.

O Mater Dei,	O Mother of God,
memento mei.	remember me.
Amen.	Amen.

34. Se la face ay pale

Guillaume Du Fay

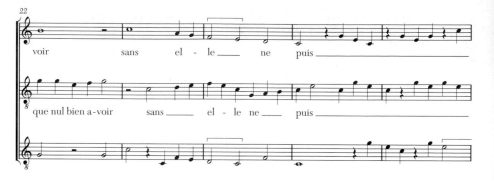

Se la face ay pale	If my face is pale,
La cause est amer	the cause is love,
C'est la principale	That is the principal reason,
Et tant m'est amer	And to love is so bitter
Amer, qu'en l'amer	that I want to throw myself
Me voudroye voir	into the sea;
Or scet bien de voir	Now, she knows well,
La belle à qui suis	The lady whom I serve,
Que nul bien avoir	that without her
Sans elle ne puis	I cannot be happy.
Se ay pesante malle	If I have a heavy load
De dueil a porter	of sorrow to bear,
Ceste amour est male	It is love that is so hard
Pour moy de porter	for me to bear;
Car soy deporter	For to enjoy oneself
Ne veult devouloir	Is something she does not allow,
Fors qu'a son vouloir	But that one
Obeisse, et puis	obeys her will,
Qu'elle a tel pooir	Because she has such power,
Sans elle ne puis	Without her I cannot be happy.

C'est la plus reale
Qu'on puist regarder
De s'amoure leiale
Ne me puis guarder
Fol sui de agarder
Ne faire devoir
D'amours recevoir
Fors d'elle, je cuij
Se ne veil douloir
Sans elle ne puis

It is the most regal bearing
One could ever see,
From loyal love
I cannot defend myself;
Foolish would I be
to look upon her
Without wanting to receive love
except from her, I think;
If I did not want to be sad,
Without her I cannot be happy.

35. **Missa se la face ay pale:** Kyrie and Gloria
Guillaume Du Fay

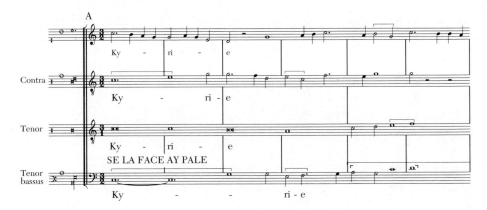

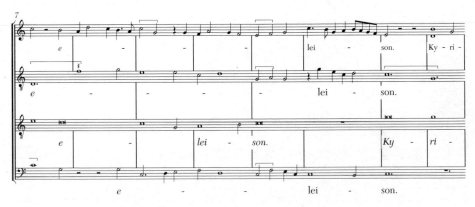

66

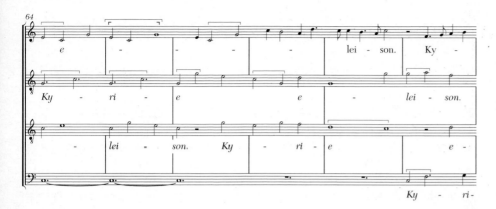

II. GLORIA IN EXELCIS DEO

Canon: Tenor ter dicitur. Primo quaelibet figura crescit in triplo, secundo in duplo, tertio ut jacet.

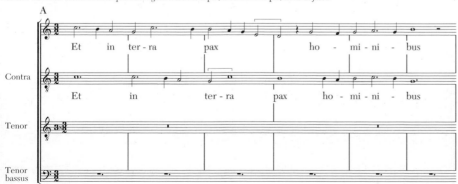

36. **Missa prolationum:** Kyrie

Johannes Ockeghem (c. 1420–1496)

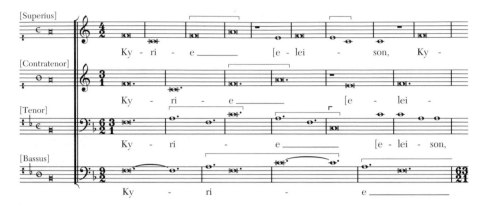

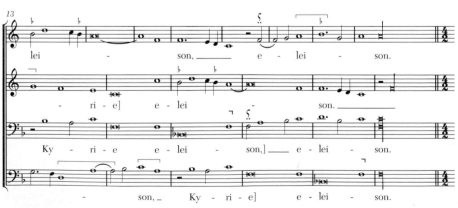

Pausans ascendit per unum tonum

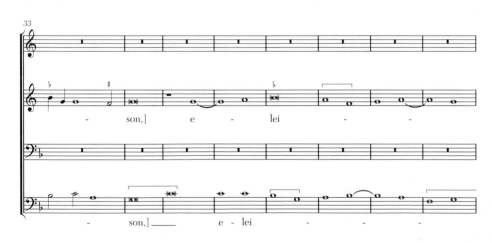

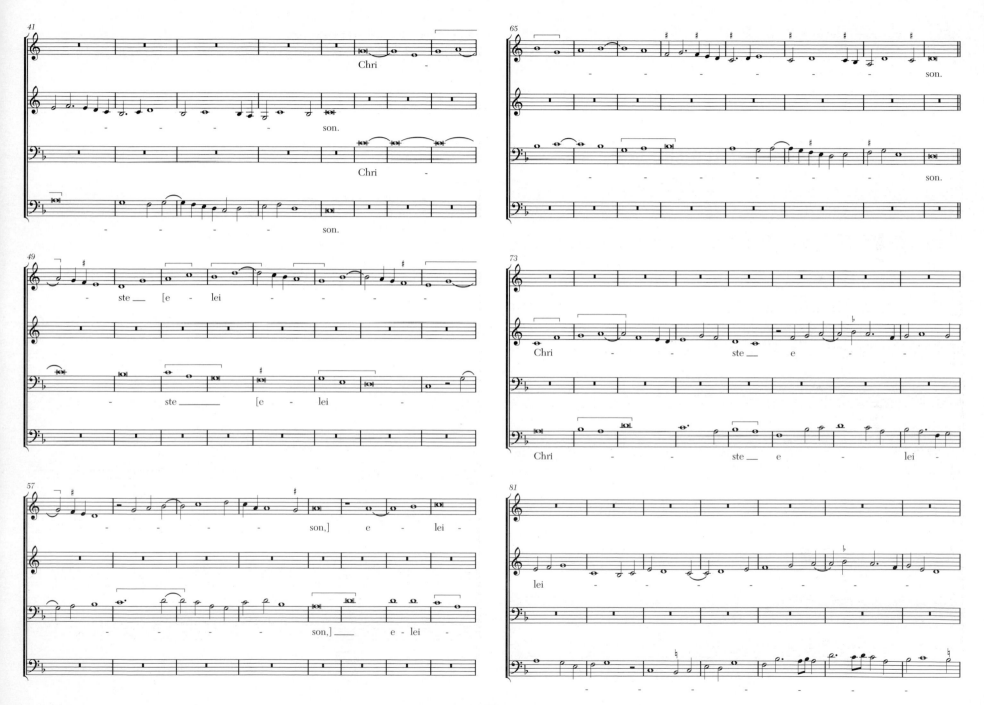

74

37. Fortuna desperata

Antoine Busnois (?) (ca. 1430–1492)

Fortuna desperata,
Iniqua e maledecta,
Che, de tal dona electa,
La fama ai denegrata.

Hopeless fortune,
Unjust and cursed,
Who has defamed the reputation
Of so distinguished a lady.

38. **Missa Fortuna desperata:** Kyrie and Agnus Dei

Josquin des Prez

Kyrie

Agnus Dei

39. Missa pange lingua: Kyrie

Josquin des Prez

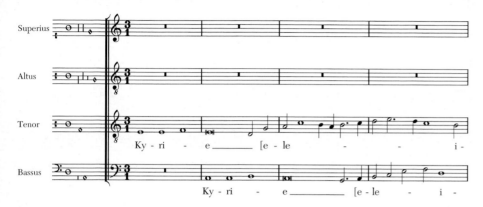

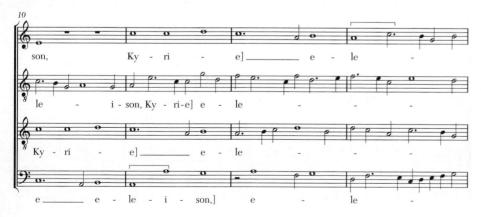

40. Absalon, fili mi

Josquin des Prez (?) or *Pierre de la Rue* (?) (ca. 1452–1518)

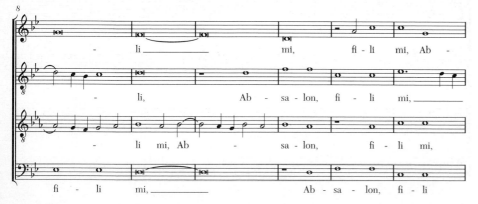

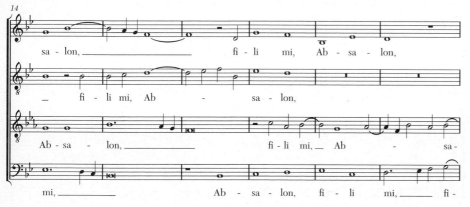

Absalon, fili mi
quis det ut moriar pro te
fili mi, Absalon?
Non viam ultra
sed descendam in infernum plorans.

Absalom, my son
Would that I had died instead of you,
My son, Absalom?
Let me live no longer,
But descend into hell, weeping.

41. Adieu ces bons vins de Lannoys

Guillaume Du Fay

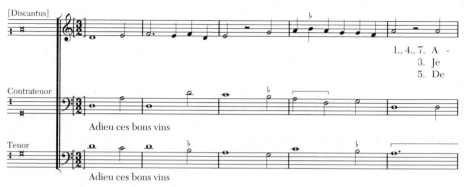

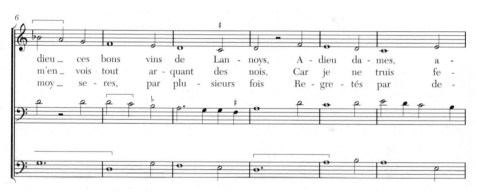

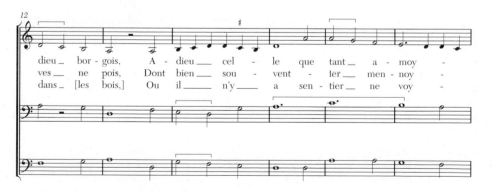

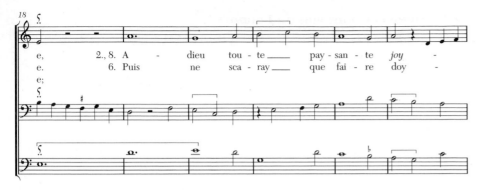

Je m'en vois tout arquant des nois,	I am going away aiming my bow at nuts,
Car je ne truis feves ne pois,	For I find neither beans nor peas,
Dont bien souvent entier mennoye.	Of which very often I bore a load.
Adieu ces bons vins de Lannoys,	Farewell these good wines of Lannoys,
Adieu dames, adieu borgois,	Farewell ladies, farewell citizens,
Adieu celle que tant amoye,	Farewell she whom I so loved.
De moy seres, par plusieurs fois	By me you will be very often
Regretés par dedans les bois,	Missed, as I go through the woods,
Ou il n'y a sentier ne voye;	Where there is no path or way;
Puis ne scaray que faire doye,	Then I shall not know what to do,
Se je ne crie a haute vois.	If I do not cry out aloud.
Adieu ces bons vins de Lannoys,	Farewell these good wines of Lannoys,
Adieu dames, adieu borgois,	Farewell ladies, farewell citizens,
Adieu celle que tant amoye,	Farewell she whom I so loved,
Adieu toute playsante joye,	Farewell every pleasing joy,
Adieu tous compaignons galois.	Farewell all my gallant companions.

Adieu ces bons vins de Lannoys,	Farewell these good wines of Lannoys,
Adieu dames, adieu borgois,	Farewell ladies, farewell citizens,
Adieu celle que tant amoye,	Farewell she whom I so loved,
Adieu toute playsante joye,	Farewell every pleasing joy,
Adieu tous compaignons galois.	Farewell all my gallant companions.

42. De tous biens plaine

Hayne van Ghizeghem (c. 1445–1485)

De tous biens plaine est ma maistresse,
Chacun lui doit tribut d'onneur.
Car assouvye est en valeur
Autant que jamais fut deesse.

En la veant j'ay tel leesse
Que c'est paradis en mon cuer.
De tous biens plaine est ma maistresse,
Chacun lui doit tribut d'onneur.

Je n'ay cure d'autre richesse
Si non d'estre son serviteur,
Et pource qu'il n'est choix milleur
En mon mot porteray sans cesse:

De tous biens plaine est ma maistresse,
Chacun lui doit tribut d'onneur.
Car assouvye est en valeur
Autant que jamais fut deesse.

Source. Laborde, fol. 62v.

My mistress is full of all good virtue,
Everyone owes her honorable tribute.
For she is accomplished in merit
As much as a goddess ever was.

When I see her I have such cheer
That paradise is in my heart.
My mistress is full of all good virtue,
Everyone owes her honorable tribute.

I have no care for other riches
Except to be her servant,
And because there is no better choice,
I carry as my unceasing motto:

My mistress is full of all good virtue,
Everyone owes her honorable tribute.
For she is accomplished in merit
As much as a goddess ever was.

43. Hélas, que devera mon coeur

Heinrich Isaac (ca. 1450–1517)

1) This note, present in all other sources, is missing in Florence 229.

2) Flat in Formschneider 1538⁹ *Trium vocum carmina* and Petrucci 1501 *Odhecaton.* On problems of *musica ficta* in this and the following two measures, see Atlas, *Cappella Guilia* 1:177.

3) Orig.: C semibreve. Emendation follows all other sources.

4) Orig.: D. Emendation follows all other sources.

Helas, que pourra devenir,	Alas, what can happen
Mon cueur, s'il ne peut parvenir	to my heart, if it cannot achieve
A celle haultaine entreprise.	that high enterprise
Où sa voulenté, s'est soubmise,	to which its will has been subjugated,
Pour mieuix sur toutes advenir?	above all else in the future?
C'est chois sans ailleurs revenir:	It is a choice without the possibility of return,
Eslicte pour temps advenir,	chosen for the future;
Avoir plaisance à sa de vise.	to have delight for its device.
Helas, . . .	Alas, etc.
Or est contraint pour l'advenir,	My future of my heart is constrained,
Car Desir l'a faict convenir,	For desire has made it appear
Qui l'a mis hors de sa franchise;	And put it beyond any sanctuary:
Et desja la cause, est commise,	And already the case is being tried,
Pour en juger à son plaisir.	For desire to judge as it pleases.
Helas, . . .	Alas, etc.

44. Hor venduto ho la speranza

Marchetto Cara (ca. 1470–1525)

Ognide - bit' ho pa - ga - to E an-cor cre - di-to m'a-van - za.

ut supra

Hor vendut'ho la speranza	I have just sold hope
Che sì cara la camprai	For which I paid so dearly,
E se ben ne ho perso assai	And if thereby I lost badly
Patientia che gli è usanza.	Well—too bad, that's the way it goes.
Ogni merce vol ventura,	Every market is risky
Io fu' in questa venturato	And in this venture I was unlucky;
Forsi mo porrò più cura	I shall learn to be more prudent
In ogni altro mio mercato.	In all my other dealings.
Ogni debito ho pagato	I have paid off all my debts
E ancor credito m'avanza.	And I have credit to spare.
Hor vendut'ho la speranza . . .	I have just sold hope . . .
Se col credito che ho anchora	If with that credit I still have
Più mi acade far contratto	I should make another contract,
Da speranza sempre in fora	I shall always exclude hope
D'ogni cosa ver a patto:	From every new agreement;
Stato è'l mal mio per un tratto	For a while it was my bad luck
Più appetito che ignoranza.	To have more ambition than sense.
Hor vendut'ho la speranza . . .	I have just sold hope . . .
O insensati ciechi amanti	O silly blind lovers.
Voi che sempre stati sete	You who are such
Di speranza gran mercanti	Great merchants of hope.
Al consiglio mio attendete	Now listen to my counsel:
In speranza non spendete	Do not trade in hope
Ché di inganno è propria stanza.	For its value is always false.
Hor vendut'ho la speranza . . .	I have just sold hope . . .
Questi falsi desleali	Those false deceitful smiles,
Risi lachryme parole	Honeyed words and tender glances
Dolci sguardi son sensali	Are negotiators
De chi speme vender suole.	For those who wish to sell.
Hor ne compri mo chi vole	Now you can buy some if you wish,
Ch'io per me compro costanza.	I, for my part, shall buy constancy.
Hor vendut'ho la speranza . . .	I have just sold hope . . .

—Translations from Peggy Forsyth,
©1984, London

45. El grillo

Josquin des Prez

89

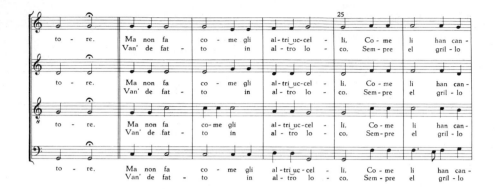

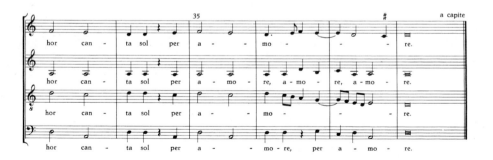

El grillo,	The cricket,
el grillo è buon cantore,	The cricket is a good singer
Che tienne longo verso,	He can sing very long
Dalle beve grillo canta	He sings all the time,
dalle, dalle, beve, beve, grillo, grillo, canta.	all the time.
El grillo,	The cricket,
el grillo è buon cantore.	The cricket is a good singer.
Ma non fa come gli altri uccelli,	But he doesn't act like the birds.
Come li han cantato un poco,	If they've sung a little bit
Van' de fatto in altro loco	They go somewhere else
	The cricket remains where he is
Sempre el grillo sta pur saldo,	
Quando la maggior è'l caldo	If the month of May is warm
Al' hor canta sol per amore.	Because he sings out of love.

90

90

46. Tant que vivray

Claudin de Sermisy (ca. 1490–1562)

Tant que vivray en aage florissant
Je serviray d'amours le roy puissant
En faictz, en ditz, en chansons et accordz;
Par plusieurs jours m'a tenu languissant,
Et puis après ma fait resjoyssant,
Car j'ay l'amour de la belle au gents corps;

Son alliance, c'est ma fiance
Son cœur est mien, le mien est sien,
Fy de tristesse, vive liesse
Puisqu'en amours a tant de biens.

Quand je la veux servir et honorer
Quand par esprit veux son nom decorer
Quand je la voie et visite souvent
Ses envieux non font que murmurer,
Mais notre amour n'en saurer moins durer
Autant ou plus en emporte le vent.
Malgré envie toute ma vie
Je serviray et chanterer
C'est la première, c'est la dernière,
Que j'ay servie et serviray.

As long as I live in my prime,
I shall serve the mighty king of Love
in deeds, in words, in songs, in harmonies.
That king made me languish a while;
but afterwards he made me rejoice,
since now I have the love of the sweetbodied
    beauty.
In her friendship is my trust,
her heart is mine, mine hers.
Away with sadness, long live gladness!—
since there are so many good things in love.

When I seek to serve and honor her,
when I seek to adorn her name with my words,
when I see and visit her—
her enviers only gossip.
But our love doesn't last any less long for that;
the wind carries their gossip and more away.
Despite their envy, I shall serve her
And sing of her all my life.
She is the first, she is the last
whom I have served and shall serve.

–Translation by Lawrence Rosenwald

47. Il bianco e dolce cigno

Jacob Arcadelt (ca. 1505–1568)

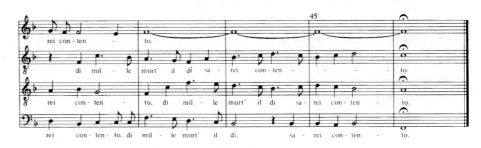

Il bianco e dolce cigno
cantando more et io
piangendo giung' al fin del viver mio.
Stran' e diversa sorte,
ch'ei more sconsolato
et io moro beato.
Morte che nel morire
m'empie di gioia tutto e di desire.
Se nel morir' altro dolor non sento
di mille mort' il dì sarei contento.

The white and gentle swan
dies singing, and I,
weeping, approach the end of my life.
Strange and diverse fates,
that he dies disconsolate
and I die happy.
Death, that in the [act of] dying
fills me wholly with joy and desire.
If in dying I feel no other pain
I would be content to die a thousand times a day.

48. Da le belle contrade d'oriente

Cipriano de Rore (1516–1565)

95

Da le belle contrade d'oriente	From the fair region of the East
Chiara e lieta s'ergea Ciprigna, et io	bright and joyful arose the morning star, and I
Fruiva in braccio al divin idol mio	in the embrace of my divine idol enjoyed
Quel piacer che non cape humana mente,	that pleasure which surpasses human understanding
Quando sentii dopo un sospir ardente:	when I heard, after an ardent sigh,
"Speranza del mio cor, dolce desio,	"Hope of my heart, sweet desire,
Te'n vai, haime, sola mi lasci, adio.	You go, alas! You leave me alone! Farewell!
Che sarà qui di me scura e dolente?	What will become of me here, gloomy and sad?
Ahi crudo Amor, ben son dubiose e corte	Alas, cruel love, how false and brief
Le tue dolcezze, poi ch'ancor ti godi	are your pleasures, for while I yet enjoy you,
Che l'estremo piacer finisca in pianto."	the ecstasy ends in tears."
Nè potendo dir più, cinseme forte,	Unable to say more, she embraced me tightly,
Iterando gl'amplessi in tanti nodi,	repeating her embraces in more entwinings,
Che giamai ne fer più l'edra o l'acanto.	than ever ivy or acanthus made.

49. Morir non può il mio cuore

Madalena Casulana (ca. 1544–after 1583)

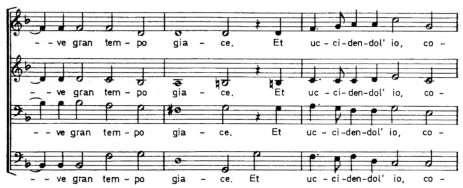

Morir non può il mio cuore,
Ucciderlo vorrei, poi che ve piace;
Ma trar non si può fuore
Dal petto vostr'ove gran tempo giace.
Et uccidendol'io come desio,
So che morreste voi morend'anch'io.

My heart cannot die,
I would like to kill it, for it would please you;
But it cannot be dragged
From your breast, where it has long lain.
And in slaying it, as I desire,
I know that you would die when I die, too.

50. Solo e pensoso

Luca Marenzio (1553 or 1554–1599)

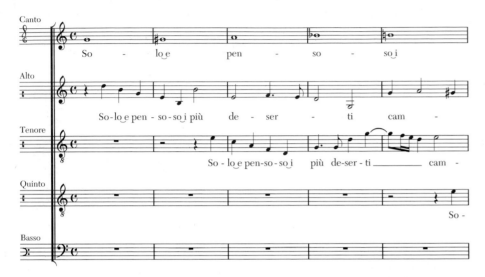

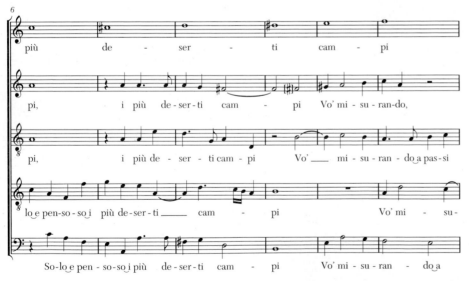

et io con lu - i, et io _ con lu - i, et io con lu - i.

i, cer-car non so et io con lu - i.

me - co, et io con lu - i, et io con lu - i.

et io con lu - i, et io con lu - i, et io con lu - i.

car non so et io con lu - i, et io con lu - i.

51. T'amo mia vita

Luzzasco Luzzaschi (1545–1607)

Prima parte

Solo e pensoso i più deserti campi
vo misurando a passi tardi e lenti,
e gl'occhi porto per fuggir intenti
dove vestiggio human l'arena stampi.
Altro schermo non trovo che mi scampi
dal manifesto accorger de le genti,
perché ne gl'atti d'allegrezza spenti
di fuor si legge com'io dentr'avampi.

Seconda parte

Sì ch'io mi cred' homai che monti e piagge
e fiumi e selve sappian di che tempre
sia la mia vita, ch'é celata altrui,
ma pur sì aspre vie né si selvagge
cercar non so ch'Amor non venga sempre
ragionando con meco, et io con lui.

       –Petrarch

Part One

Alone and pensive through the most deserted fields
I go with measured steps, dragging and slow
And my eyes intently watch in order to flee
From any spot where the trace of man the sand imprints,
No other defense do I find to escape
From the plain knowledge of people,
Because in my actions, of joy devoid,
From without one may read how I blaze within.

Part Two

Yet I believe that hills and vales,
Rivers and forests know of my life and
What is hidden from others.
For no matter how arduous and wild a path
I seek, Amor always appears
Speaking to me, and I with him.

"T'amo mia vita," la mia cara vita
dolcemente me dice; e in questa sola
si soave parola
Par mi trasformi lietamente il core.
O voce di dolcezza e di diletto.
Prendila tosta Amore,
stampala nel mio petto,
spiri dunque per lei l'anima mia.
"T'amo mia vita," la mia vita sia.

"I love you my life," my dearest life
softly tells me; and with these
such gentle words
my heart is joyfully transformed.
O voice of sweetness and delight.
Take it soon, Love,
stamp it upon my breast
so that I may breathe only for her.
"I love you my life," be my life.

52. Matona mia cara

Orlande de Lassus (1530 or 1532–1594)

110

Matona, mia cara,	O my good lady,
Mi follere canzon,	I want to sing a song
Cantar sotto finestra,	Below your window
Lantze buon compagnon,	Lancer good companion
Don don don, di ri di ri don don don don,	Don don don . . .
Don don don, di ri di ri don don don don.	
Ti prego m'as coltare,	I beg you listen to me,
Che mi cantar de don,	Because I sing good,
E mi ti foler bene,	And I want you,
Come greco e capon,	Like a Greek wants his capon.
Don don don . . .	Don don don . . .
Com' andar alle cazze,	When I go to the hunting,
Cazze, cazzar con le falcon,	To the hunting with the falcon,
Mi ti portar beccazze	I bring you a woodcock
Grasse come rognon.	So fat as a kidney.
Don don don . . .	Don don don . . .
Si mi non saper dire	I do not know how to say
Tante belle rason,	The beautiful things;
Petrarcha mi non saper,	Petrarch I do not know,
Ne fonte d'Helicon.	Nor the fount of Helicon,
Don don don . . .	Don don don . . .
Si ti mi foller bene,	But if you love me,
Mi non esser poltron,	I am not a fool,
Mi ficcar tutta notte,	I make love all night,
Urtar, urtar come monton,	Pushing like a ram.
Don don don . . .	Don don don . . .

53. Innsbruck, ich muss dich lassen

Isaac

2. Groß Leid muß ich jetz tragen,
das ich allein tu klagen
dem liebsten Bühlen mein.
Ach Lieb, nun laß mich Armen
im Herzen dein erbarmen,
daß ich von dann muß sein!

3. Mein Trost ob allen Weiben,
dein tu ich ewig pleiben,
stet, treu, der Ehren frumm.[4]
Nun muß[5] dich Gott bewahren,
in aller Tugend sparen[6]
bis daß ich wiederkumm!

1) = Innsbruck 2) = (wieder) zu erlangen 3) = im fremden Land 4) = tüchtig, rechtschaffen 5) = möge 6) = erhalten

111

Innsbruck, ich muss dich lassen,
ich fahr dahin mein Strassen,
in fremde Land dahin.
Mein Freud ist mir genommen,
die ich nit weiss bekommen,
wo ich im Elend bin.

Gross Leid muss ich jetzt tragen,
das ich allein tu klagen
dem liebsten Buhlen mein.
Ach Lieb, nun lass mich Armen
im Herzen dein erbarmen,
dass ich muss dannen sein.

Mein Trost ob allen Weiben,
dein tu ich ewig bleiben,
stet treu, der Ehren fromm.
Nun muss dich Gott bewahren,
in aller Tugend sparen,
bis dass ich wiederkomm.

Innsbruck, I must leave you
I am going on my way
into a foreign land.
My joy is taken from me,
I know not how to regain it,
while in such misery.

I must now endure great pain
which I confide only
to my dearest love.
O beloved, find pity
in your heart for me,
that I must part from you.

My comfort above all other women,
I shall always be yours,
forever faithful in honor true.
May the good Lord protect you
and keep you in your virtue
for me, till I return.

N. Greenberg and P. Maynard

54. Zwischen Berg und tiefem Tal
Ludwig Senfl (ca. 1486–1542 or 1543)

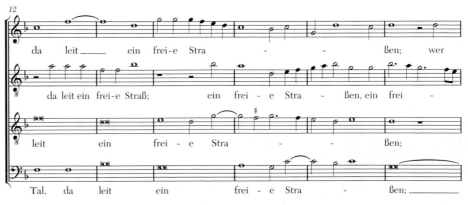

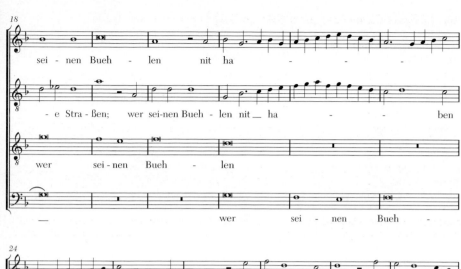

Zwischen Berg und tiefem Tal
Da leit ein freie Straßen.
Wer seinen Buehlen nit haben mag,
Der mueß ihn fahren lassen.

Fahr' hin, fahr' hin, du hast die Wahl,
ich kann mich dein wohl massen.
Im Jahr sind noch viel langer Tag,
Glück is in allen Gassen.

Between the mountain and the deep valley
There lies an open road.
Whoever doesn't want to keep his love
Must let that love go.

Go on, go on! You have the choice.
I can well tell what you're up to.
There's many a long day left in the year,
Good fortune can be found in every alley.

113

55. Silberweise

Hans Sachs (1494–1576)

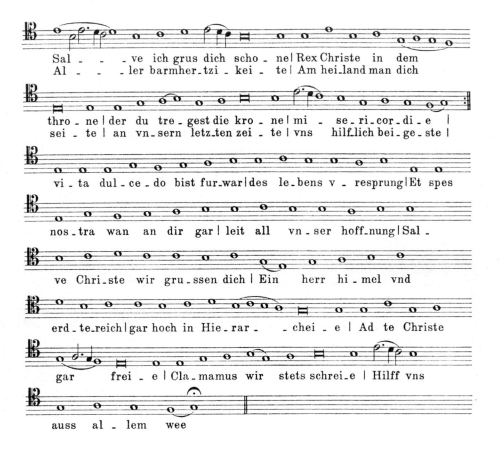

Salve ich grus dich schone
Rex Christe in dem throne
der du tregest die krone
misericordie

Aller barmhertzikeite
Am heiland man dich seite
an vnsern letzten zeite
vns hilflich beigeste

vita dulcedo
bist furwar des lebens vresprung
Et spes nostra
wan an dir gar leit all vnser hoffnung

Salve Christe wir grussen dich
Ein herr himel vnd erdtereich
gar hoch in Hierarcheie
Ad te Christe gar freie
Clamamus wir stets schreie
Hilff vns auss allem wee

Hail! I greet you most fittingly.
O Christ, King on the throne,
you who wear the crown,
have mercy.

You of all mercy,
you were proclaimed the savior.
In our ultimate days
may you support us with your help!

Life and sweetness,
you are indeed the source of life.
And also our hope,
for in you lies all of our hope.

Hail, O Christ, we greet you,
one Lord in the kingdom of heaven and earth,
most high in the celestial hierarchy.
To you, O Christ, most willingly we cry,
continually we cry.
Deliver us from our misery.

—Translation by Salvatore Calomino

56. Al amor quiero vencer

Luis Milán (ca. 1500–after 1561)

A. Molto Lento

1. Al a— mor quie— ro ven— cer mas quien po— dra.
4. Quien tu— vies— se tal po— der mas quien po— dra. Qu'e—lla con su

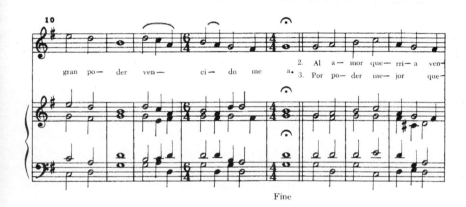

gran po— der ven— ci— do me a.
2. Al a— mor que— rri— a ven—
3. Por po— der me— jor que—

Fine

cer y con bien ser del ven—ci— do.
rer pa— ra ser me— jor que—ri— do.

D.C. al Fine

B. Allegro Moderato

1. Al a— mor quie— ro ven— cer mas quien po—
4. Quien tu— vies— se tal po— der mas quien po—

dra.
dra. Qu'e—lla con su gran po—

der ven— ci— do me ha.

Fine

115

Al amor quiero vencer
mas quien podrá?
Quella con su gran poder
vencido me ha.
Al amor querria vencer
y con bien ser del vencido,
por poder mejor querer,
para ser mejor querido.
Quien tuviesse tal poder,
mas quien podrá?
Quella con su gran poder
vencido me ha.

I wish to conquer Love
But how can it be done?
She has overcome me
with her great power.
I wish to overcome Love
and to be overcome,
To love better
And be better loved.
Oh! to have such power!
But whoever could?
She has overcome me
with her great power.

–Translation by Nicki Kennedy

57. Now Is the Month of Maying

Thomas Morley (1557–1602)

58. Come, Heavy Sleep

John Dowland (1563–1626)

59. Ein feste Burg ist unser Gott

Johann Walter (1496–1570)

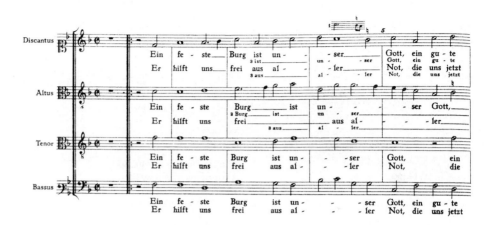

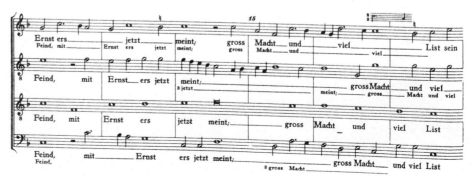

2. Come, shadow of my end, and shape of rest,
Allied to death, child to this black-faced night,
Come thou and charm these rebels in my breast,
Whose waking fancies doth my mind affright.
O come, sweet sleep, come or I die for ever;
Come ere my last sleep come, or come never.

Ein feste Burg ist unser Gott,
ein gute Wehr und Waffen.
Er hilft uns frei aus aller Not,
die uns jetzt hat betroffen.
Der alt böse Feind,
mit Ernst ers jetzt meint;
gross Macht und viel List
sein grausam Rüstung ist;
auf Erd is nicht seins Gleichen.

A mighty fortress is our God,
A trusty shield and weapon;
He helps us free from ev'ry need
That hath us now o'ertaken.
The old evil foe
Now means deadly woe:
Deep guile and great might
are his dread arms in fight,
On earth is not his equal.

60. Verily, Verily I Say Unto You

Thomas Tallis (1505–1585)

St. John 6, vv. 53-56.

121

61. Sing Joyfully Unto God

William Byrd (1542–1623)

123

124

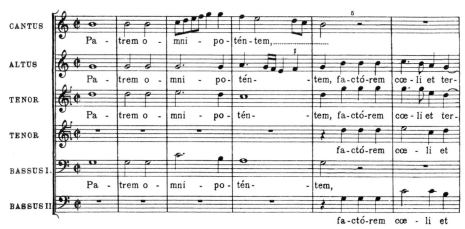

62. **Missa Papae Marcelli:** Credo

Giovanni Pierluigi da Palestrina (1525 or 1526–1594)

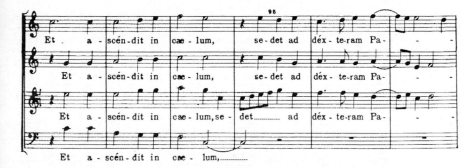

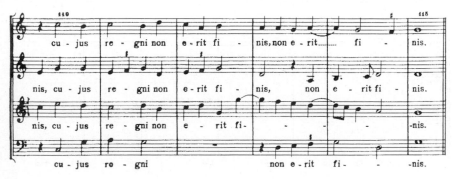

63. Diferencias sobre el canto de la Dama le demanda

Antonio Cabezón (1510–1566)

64. Ricercar

Francesco Spinacino (fl. early 16th century)

133

65. Ricercar del duodecimo tuono

Andrea Gabrieli (1532 or 1533–1585)

Canto
Alto
Tenore
Basso

66. Fantasia chromatica

Jan Pieterszoon Sweelinck (1562–1621)

67. Dances from **Het derde musyck boexken**
Tielman Susato (ca. 1500–ca. 1561)

La morisque

Ronde VI

Saltarelle

68. Dances from **Terpsichore**

Michael Praetorius (1571–1621)

XXXII. à 4.
La Bouree.

CCX. à 5.

69. Prophetiae Sibyllarum
Orlande de Lassus

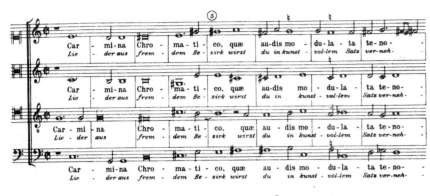

Carmina chromatico quae audis modulata
  tenore
Haec sunt illa quibus nostrae olim arcana salutis
Bis senae intrepido cecinerunt ore Sybillae.

These are songs which proceed chromatically.
They are the poems in which the twelve
Sibyls, one after the other, once sang the hidden
mysteries of our salvation.

70. Cum essem parvulus
Orlande de Lassus

142

Prima pars
Cum essem parvulus,
loquebar ut parvulus,
sapiebam ut parvulus,
cogitam ut parvulus.
Quando autem factus sum vir,
evacuavi quae erant parvuli.

Videmus nunc per speculum in aenigmate,
tunc autem facie ad faciem.

Seconda pars
Nunc cognosco ex parte,
tunc autem cognoscam sicut
et cognitus sum.

Nunc autem manent fides, spes, caritas,
tria haec, maior autem horum
est caritas.

Part One
When I was a child,
I spoke as a child,
I understood as a child,
I thought as a child;
but when I became a man,
I put away childish things.

We see now a riddle through a mirror
[King James: As through a glass darkly],
But then face to face.

Part Two
Now I know in part,
but then I shall know even as also
I am known.

And now abideth faith, hope, love,
these three; but the greatest of these
is love.

I Corinthians 13:11–13

71. **Dunque fra torbid' onde** from **Il Canto d'Arione**

Giacopo Peri (1561–1633)

147

148

(1) [notation] (2) [notation] (3) [notation]

149

Arione

Dunque fra torbide onde
Gli ultimi miei sospir manderà fuore,
Ecco gentil con tuoi suavi accenti:
Raddoppia i miei tormenti;
Ahi, lacrime, ahi dolore,
Ahi morte troppo acerba e troppo dura.
Ma deh, chi,
O di Terra o di Cielo
S'a torto io mi querelo:
E s'a ragion mi doglio;
Movetevi a pietà del mio cordoglio.

Arion

Thus over troubled waters
I shall exhale my final sighs.
Gentle Echo, with your tender accents,
Redouble my torments,
O tears, O pains!
O death, too bitter and too hard!
Oh, who on the Earth or in the Sky
Would accuse me
Of a wrongful complaint?
And if I grieve with reason,
Have pity on me in my grief.

72. Sfogava con le stelle

Giulio Caccini (1545–1618)

151

Sfogava con le stelle	He vented to the stars
Un inferno d'amore	An inferno of love
Sotto notturno cielo il suo dolore,	Under the night sky, grieving,
E dicea fisso in loro:	Saying to them:
O immagini belle	"O lovely images
Dell'idol mio ch'adoro,	Of my adored one,
Si come a me mostrate,	Just as you reveal to me,
Mentre così splendete,	By shining so brightly,
La sua rara beltate,	Her rare beauty,
Così mostraste a lei,	Show to her as well
Mentre cotanto ardete,	My intense passion,
I vivi ardori miei.	My burning love.
La fareste co'l vostro aureo sembiante	Make her, with your golden gleam,
Pietosa sì, come me fate amante.	Pity me, as you have made me love her."

73. Al fonte, al prato

Giulio Caccini

Al fonte, al prato,	To the spring, to the meadow,
Al bosco, a l'ombra,	To the woods, to the shade,
Al fresco fiato	To the fresh breeze
Ch'il caldo sgombra,	That disperses the heat,
Pastor correte;	Shepherds, run;
Ciascun ch'a sete,	Let him who is thirsty,
Ciascun ch'è stanco	Let him who is weary,
Ripos' il fianco.	Rest his flanks.
Fugga la noia,	Away with boredom,
Fugga il dolore,	Away with grief,
Sol riso e gioia,	Let only laughter and joy
Sol caro amore.	And love be among us
Nosco soggiorni	In our sojourns,
Ne' lieti giorni,	In these happy days,
Nè s'odan mai	Never let there be heard
Querele o lai.	Quarrels or laments.
Ma dolce canto	But sweet song
Di vaghi uccelli	Of pretty birds
Pe 'l verde manto	Through the green mantle
Degli arbuscelli	Of the trees
Risuoni sempre	Shall echo always
Con nuovi tempre,	With new timbres,
Mentre ch'a l'onde	And like the waves
Ecco risponde.	It thus responds.
E mentre alletta	And while she charms,
Quanto più puote	As best she can,
La giovinetta	The young maiden, singing
Con rozze note	With rough notes
Il sonno dolce,	To the sweet sleep
Ch'il caldo molce,	That soothes the heat,
E noi pian piano	Let us ever so quietly
Con lei cantiano.	Sing with her.

74. Cruda Amarilli

Claudio Monteverdi (1567–1643)

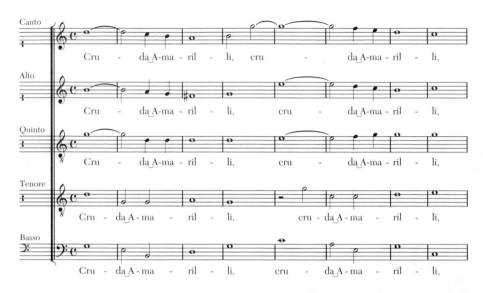

Cruda Amarilli
che col nome ancora
d'amar, ahi lassa, amaramente insegni;
Amarilli, del candido ligustro
più candida e più bella,
ma dell'aspido sordo
e più sorda e più fera e più fugace,
poi che col dir t'offendo,
i' mi morrò tacendo.

(B. Guarini)

Cruel Amaryllis,
who with your name still
Teaches us, alas, a bitter lesson of love;
Amaryllis, whiter and more beautiful
Than the white privet blossom,
But also more stealthy than the adder
More stealthy, and wilder, and more elusive,
If in saying this I offend you
I shall go to my death in silence.

75. T'amo mia vita

Monteverdi

Claudio Monteverdi

"T'amo mia vita," la mia cara vita
dolcemente me dice; e in questa sola
si soave parola
Par mi trasformi lietamente il core.
O voce di dolcezza e di diletto.
Prendila tosta Amore,
stampala nel mio petto,
spiri dunque per lei l'anima mia.
"T'amo mia vita," la mia vita sia.

"I love you my life," my dearest life
softly tells me; and with these
such gentle words
my heart is joyfully transformed.
O voice of sweetness and delight.
Take it soon, Love,
stamp it upon my breast
so that I may breathe only for her.
"I love you my life," be my life.

76. Zefiro torna e di soavi accenti
Monteverdi

164

Zefiro torna e di soavi accenti
L'aer fa grato e'l piè discioglie a l'onde,

E mormorando tra le verdi fronde
Fa danzar al bel suon su'l prato i fiori,
Inghirlandato il crin Fillide e Clori
Note temprando amor care e gioconde
E da monti e da valli ime e profonde
Raddopian l'armonia gli antri canori.
Sorge più vaga in ciel l'aurora e'l sole

Sparge più luci d'or, più puro argento
Fregia di Teti il bel ceruleo manto.
Sol io per selve abbandonate e sole
L'ardor di due begli occhi e'l mio tormento.
Come vuol mia ventura hor piango, hor canto.

       –Ottavio Rinuccini

The west wind returns and with soft accents
makes the air gentle and releases swift-footed
 waves,
and murmuring among the green branches
makes the flowers dance at its lovely sound
and curls round the hair of Phyllis and Clori,
love giving rise to fond and joyful song,
and from mountains and valleys low and deep,
the sonorous caves reecho the music.
The dawn rises more lovely in the sky, and the
 sun
scatters more golden rays, and a purer silver
decorates Teti's beautiful sky blue coat.
Only I in the lonely, deserted forest—
the fire of two bright eyes is my torment.
As my fortune wills, I weep, then sing.

77. Lasciatemi qui solo

Francesca Caccini (1587–ca. 1640)

Lasciatemi qui solo (author unknown; last line of each stanza echoes a line from Rinuccini's lament for the title character in *L'Arianna*, 1608)

Lasciatemi qui solo
Tornate augelli al nido
Mentre l'anim'e'l duolo
Spiro su questo lido.
Altri meco non vòglio
Ch'un freddo scoglio e'l mio
fatal martire.
Lasciatemi morire.

Dolcissime sirene,
Ch'en si pietoso canto
Radollcite mie pene
Fate soave il pianto
Movete il nuoto altronde
Togliete all'onde i crudi
sdegni e l'ire
Lasciatemi morire.

Placidissimi venti
Tornate al vostro speco
Sol miei duri lamenti
Chieggio che restin meco.
Vostri sospir non chiamo
Solingo bramò i miei dolor
finire.
Lasciatemi morire.

Felicissimi amanti
Tornate al bel diletto
Fere occh'o notanti
Fuggiti'il mesto aspetto
Sol dolcezza di morte
Apra la porte all'ultimo
languire.
Lasciatemi morire.

Avarissimi lumi
Che su'l morir versate
Amarissimi fiumi
Tard'è vostra pietate.
Già mi sento mancare
O luci avar'e tarde al mio
conforto.
Già sono e sangu'e smorto.

Leave me here alone.
Return, birds, to your nest
While I breathe out my spirit
and sorrow on this beach.
I want no other with me
But a cold rock and my fatal
suffering.
Let me die.

Sweetest sirens,
Who in such piteous song
Sweeten my pains
(And) make gentle weeping,
Move your swimming elsewhere.
Remove from the waves cruel
scorn and angers.
Let me die.

Most placid winds,
Return to your cave.
Only my harsh laments
Do I ask to remain with me.
I call not on your sighs.
Solitary, I long for my sorrow
to end.
Let me die.

Happiest lovers,
Return to sweet delight.
Fierce, observant eyes,
Flee this sad sight.
Only the sweetness of death
Opens the door to the ultimate
pleasure.
Let me die.

Greediest of eyes
That shed over my death
The bitterest of streams,
Your pity is late.
Already I feel faint.
O greedy eyes, you come too
late to comfort me.
I am already both bleeding and dying.
–Translation by Suzanne Cusick

78. Tradimento!

Barbara Strozzi (1619–1664)

167

siero di-ce d'es-ser-ne con - ten - to. Tra-di-

men-to, ⟨tra-di-men-to,⟩ tra-di-men-to, ⟨tra-di-men-to!⟩

La spe-ran-za per le-gar

- mi a gran co-se mi lu-sin - ga, s'io le

cre - do av-vien che strin

- ga lac-ci sol, lac-ci sol da in-ca-te-nar

- mi, lac-ci sol _____ da in-ca-te-nar

- mi. Mio co-re al-l'ar-mi, al-l'ar-mi, al-l'ar-mi! S'in-con-tri l'in-

fi-da si pren-da s'uc-ci-da, ⟨s'in-con-tri l'in-fi-da si pren-da s'uc-

ci-da,⟩ al-l'ar-mi, ⟨al-l'ar-mi,⟩ al-l'ar-mi, al-l'ar - mi, s'in

con-tri l'in-fi-da si pren-da s'uc-ci-da su pre-sto, ⟨su pre-sto!⟩

e pe-ri-glio - so, e pe-ri-glio - so, e pe-ri-glio - so

 62

o - gni mo-men-to, __ o - gni mo-men - to. Tra-di-men-to, ⟨tra-di-

65

men-to,⟩ tra-di-men-to, ⟨tra-di-men-to, tra-di-men-to, tra-di-men-to!⟩

Tradimento!	Betrayal!
Amore e la Speranza voglion farmi prigioniero	Love and Hope want to make me their prisoner
E a tal segno il mal s'avanza	And my sickness is so advanced
Ch'ho scoperto ch'il pensiero	That I realize I am happy
Dice d'esserne contento.	Just thinking of it.
Tradimento!	Betrayal!
La Speranza per legarmi	Hope, to bind me,
A gran cose mi lusinga	Entices me with great things.
S'io le credo avvien che stringa	The more I believe what she says
Lacci sol da incatenarmi.	The tighter she ties the knots that imprison me.
Mio core all' armi, s'incontri l'infida	To arms, my heart, to arms against the unfaithful one.
Si prenda s'uccida, su presto!	Take her and kill her, hurry!
E periglioso ogni momento	Every moment is dangerous.
Tradimento!	Betrayal!

79. Enfin la beauté que j'adore

Etienne Moulinié (ca. 1600–after 1669)

En - fin la beau - té que j'a - do - re __ Me fait cognoistre en son re - tour,

tour, Qu'el - le veut que

(1) ♩ dans la tablature.

169

Enfin la beauté que j'adore
Me fait cognoistre en son retour,
Qu'elle veut que je voye encore
Ces yeux pour qui je meurs d'amour.
Mais puis que je revoy la beauté qui m'enflame,

Sortez mes desplaisirs, hostez vous de mon ame.

Le ciel voyant que son absence
M'oste tout mon contentement,
Octroye à ma persévérance
La fin de mon cruel tourment.
Mais puis que je revoy . . .

Mes maux changés vous en délices,
Mon cœur, arretes vos douleurs,
Amour bannissez mes supplices,
Mes yeux ne versez plus de pleurs.
Et puis que je revoy.

At last the beauty I worship
Lets me know upon her return
That she still wishes me to see
Those eyes for which I die of love.
But since I see again the beauty which
      consumes me,
Be gone, troubles, leave my soul.

Heaven, seeing that her absence
Deprives me of my happiness,
Grants, because of my perseverance,
The end of my cruel torment.
But since I see . . .

My wounds, turn yourselves into delights.
My heart, stop your aching.
Love, banish my tortures.
Eyes, shed no more tears.
And since I see . . .

–Translation by Ellen Hargis and Candice Smith

80. Orfeo, Act II, excerpt
Monteverdi

Fu sonato questo ritornello di dentro da cinque viole da braccio, un contrabasso, due Clavicembani e tre chitaroni.

Ritornello

(Allegro, ma non troppo)

ORFEO

Vi ri_cor_da o bo_schi ombro_si Vi ri_cor_da o boschi om_

(Più tranquillo)

_bro_si de'miei lungh'aspri tor_menti quando i sassi ai miei la_men_ti rispondean fat_ti pie_

_to_si Vi ri_cor_da o bo_sch'om_bro_si, vi ri_cor_da o bo_sch'om_

171

172

1) Manca l' indicazione del personaggio ma è un Pastore

175

176

100 far - ne u - na ghirlan-da a le sue chio-me, quand'an-gue in-si-dio-so ch'e-

111 -mar tentando li spir-ti in lei smarri-ti con l'onda fresca e con possen-ti carmi, ma

102 -ra fra l'erbe asco-so, le pun-se un piè con ve-le-no-so den-te.

113 nul-la val-se ahi las-sa ch'el-la i langui-di lu-mi alquan-to apren-

104 Ed ec-co immanti-nente sco-lo-rir-si il bel vi-so

3 4 3

116 -do e te chiamando Orfe-o, Or-fe-o Do-po un gra-ve so-

106 e nei suoi lumi sparir que lam-pi ond'ella al sol fea scor-no al-

119 -spi-ro spi-rò fra queste braccia ed io rima-si piena il cor di pie-

(♮)

109 -l'hor noi tut-te sbi-got-ti-te e me-ste le fummo intor-no ri-chia-

122 -ta-de e di spa-ven-to.

PASTORE

Ahi ca-so acer-bo ahi fat'empio e crude-le. Ahi

CHORO

(Andante)

Vi ricorda o boschi ombrosi
Vi ricorda o boschi ombrosi
de'miei lungh'aspri tormenti
quando i sassi ai miei lamenti
rispondean fatti pietosi
Vi ricorda o bosch'ombrosi,
vi ricorda o bosch'ombrosi.

Dite all'hor non vi sembrai
Dite al l'hor non vi sembrai
più d'ogn'altro sconsolato
Hor fortuna ha stil cangiato
et ha volto in festa i guai
Dite all'hor non vi sembrai
più d'ogn'altro sconsolato.

Vissi già mesto e dolente,
vissi già mesto e dolente
Hor gioisco e quegli affanni
che sofferti ho per tant'anni
fan più caro il ben presente.
Vissi già mesto e dolente,
vissi già mesto e dolente.

Sol per te bella Euridice,
sol per te bella Euridice,
benedico il mio tormento,
dopo il duol viè più contento
dopo il mal viè più felice.
Sol per te bella Euridice,
sol per te bella Euridice.

Mira deh mira Orfeo
che d'ogni intorno
ride il bosco e ride il prato.
Segui pur col plettr'aurato
d'addolcir l'aria in si beato giorno.
Ahi caso acerbo
Ahi fat'empio e crudele
Ahi stelle ingiuriose
ahi ciel avaro.

Qual suon dolente il lieto di perturba?
Lassa dunque debb'io mentre
Orfeo con sue note il ciel consola
con le parole mie passangli il core.
Questa è Silvia gentile
dolcissima compagna della bell'Euridice
O quanto e in vista dolorosa
hor che sia deh sommi

Woodland groves do ye remember,
woodland groves do ye remember
all my cruel bitter torments,
when the rocks heard my lamenting
and in pity gave me answer?
Woodland groves do ye remember?
Woodland groves do ye remember?

Come reply, more broken hearted,
Come reply, more broken hearted
did ye e'er behold a lover?
Now has fortune tuned her lute strings
and has turned to joy my sorrow!
Come reply, more broken hearted
did ye e'er behold a lover?

I was full of grief and sorrow,
I was full of grief and sorrow,
but rejoice now in my gladness.
By so many years of sighing
is my joy today perfected.
I was full of grief and sorrow,
I was full of grief and sorrow.

In thy favours, fair Eurydice,
in thy favours, fair Eurydice,
do I bless my bitter torments.
After grief is joy thrice hallow'd,
after evil good thrice blessed.
In thy favours, fair Eurydice,
do I bless my bitter torments.

Marvel, yea marvel, Orpheus,
that all around thee
laughs the forest, laugh the meadows!
Haste thee then with plectrum of gold
to soothe the zephyrs of this blessed morning.
Ah bitter sorrow!
Ah fate cruel and impious!
Ah stars of ill designing!
ah heav'n voracious!

What cries of mourning disturb this our gladness?
Ah me! Wherefore must I now
while with song all the heav'n Orpheus rejoiceth
with cruel tidings rend his heart asunder.
This is Sylvia most gentle,
the sweetest of the comrades of the fair Eurydice.
Heavy her eyes with sorrow!
Whate'er her news turn not from us,

Dei non torcete da noi benigno il guardo.
Pastor lasciate il canto
ch'ogni nostra allegrezza in doglia è volta.
D'onde vieni? ove vai? . . .
Ninfa che porti?
A te ne vengo Orfeo
messaggera infelice
di caso più infelice e più funesto
la tua bella Euridice.
Ohimè che odo?
La tua diletta sposa è morta.
Ohimè.
In un fiorito prato
con l'altre sue compagne
giva cogliendo fiori
per farne una ghirlanda a le sue chiome,
quand'angue insidioso ch'era fra l'erbe ascoso,

le punse un piè con velenoso dente.
Ed ecco
immantinente scolorirsi il bel viso
e nei suoi lumi sparir que lampi
ond'ella al sol fea scorno
all'hor noi tuttesbigottite e meste
le fummo intorno richiamar tentando

li spirti in lei smarriti
con l'onda fresca e con possenti carmi,
ma nulla valse ahi lassa
ch'ella i languidi lumi
alquanto aprendo e te chiamando
Orfeo, Orfeo
Dopo un grave sospiro
spirò fra queste braccia
ed io rimasi piena il cor di pietade
e di spavento.
Ahi caso acerbo
ahi fat'empio e crudele.
Ahi stelle ingiuriose,
ahi ciel avaro.

A l'amara novella
rassembra l'infelice
un muto sasso
che per troppo dolor non può dolersi;
Ahi ben havrebbeuncor di Tigre o d'Orsa
chi non sentisse del tuo mal pietate,
privo d'ogni tuo ben misero amante.

O gods in heaven above your kind regarding.
Fair youth, have done with singing,
For today our rejoicing is turned to mourning.
Whence dost thou come? Whither go?
Nymph, tell thy tidings!
To thee, Orpheus, I come,
cruel tidings I bear thee:
a tragedy of horror dark and grievous;
For thy lovely Eurydice
Alas, what hear I?
Thy well beloved bride is dead.
Woe's me!
As through the meads she wandered
with three of her companions
gathering woodland blossoms,
Wherewith to wreath a garland for her tresses,
A treacherous serpent, which in the grass was
    lurking,
Within her buried his envenom'd fangs.
And lo!
the wine-red hue of life deserts her fair visage,
and from her eyes banisheth that lustre
which made the sun ashamed,
and we, our horror and dismay withstanding,
around her stood and with cool water bathing
    her forehead,
strove to recall the ebbing spirit,
and loudly heav'n invoked,
but all in vain, ah sorrow!
For then her languid eyes
a little opening she cried upon thee
"Orpheus, my Orpheus!"
With a last deep sigh
within these arms she perish'd,
and I remained of pity and terror
a victim spellbound.
Ah bitter sorrow!
Ah fate cruel and impious!
Ah stars of ill designing!
Ah heav'n voracious!

At these tidings so grievous
he all unhappy stands like a
rock in silence.
Grief so bitter as his no tongue can utter.
Ah, he must have a heart of bear or tiger
who would not pity feel for thy affliction,
of ev'ry joy bereft, star crossed lover!

Tu se' morta se' morta mia vita
ed io respiro,
tu se' da me partita,
se'da me partita per mai più,
mai più non tornare ed io rimango,
no, no,
che se i versi alcuna cosa ponno,
n'andrò sicuro a più profondi abissi
e intenerito il cor del Re de l'ombre
meco trarrotti a riveder le stelle,

O se ciò negherammi empio destino,
rimarrò teco in compagnia di morte
a dio terra a dio cielo
e Sole, a Dio.

Ahi caso acerbo, Ahi fat'empio e crudele,
Ahi stelle ingiuriose ahi cielo avaro.
Non si fidi huom mortale
Di ben caduco e frale
che tosto fugge, e spesso
a gran fati ca
il precipizio è presso.

Thou art dead, art dead my life,
and I am living.
Thou now from me art sever'd,
sever'd from me now forever.
Thou mayest return never and I shall remain?
No, No!
If there still lies virtue in my singing,
I will go down to the most deep abysses,
I will soften the heart of the king of shadows,
and I will bring thee once more to see the star
    light,
or if destiny impious this denies me,
I will remain there with thee in death abiding.
Farewell earth, farewell sky,
and Sun, farewell.

Ah bitter sorrow! Ah fate cruel and impious!
Ah stars of ill designing! Ah heav'n voracious!
Bring not thy gifts O mortal,
to Fortune's transient portal;
Soon will thy goddes frustrate thee
Wheree'er thou climbest,
Lo! yawning gulfs await thee.

81. L'incoronazione di Poppea, Act I, Scenes 2 and 3
Monteverdi

Scena seconda
Ottone e due Soldati, che si risvegliano
Soldati di Nerone si svegliano, e da'patimenti sofferti in quella notte malediscono gl'amori di
Poppea, e di Nerone, e mormorano della corte.

Scene II
Otho and two soldiers
*Nero's soldiers awake; while complaining about the discomforts of the previous night, they curse
the love of Poppaea and Nero, and gossip about the court.*

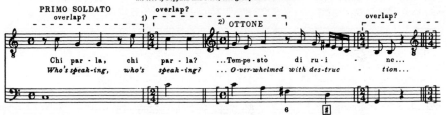

1) The irregular barring at the beginning of this scene would seem to indicate overlapping and interruption for the portrayal of
the soldier's waking exclamations.
2) The two interrupted fragments of Ottone's parting speech which Monteverdi(?) overlapped into Scene ii are in *alto* clef in N and
V, as is his entire part in Act III in V (see Preface).

181

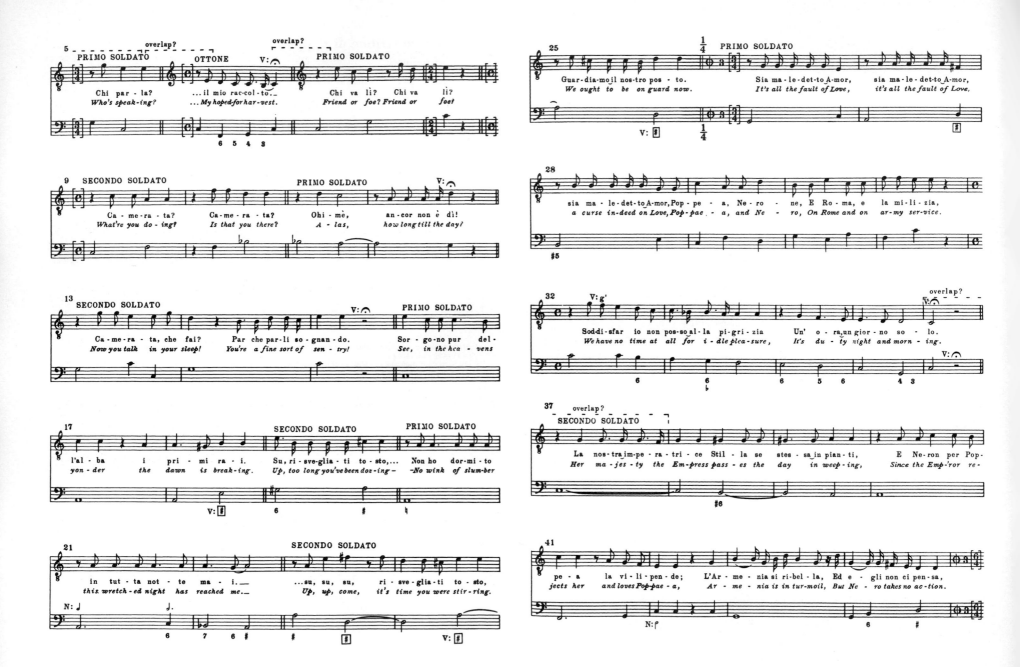

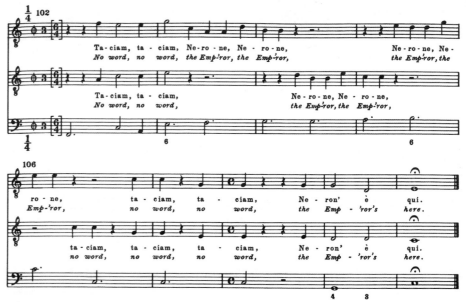

Scena terza

Poppea, Nerone

Poppea, e Nerone escono al far del giorno amorosamente abbracciati, prendendo commiato l'uno dall'altro con tenerezze affettuose.

Scene III

Poppaea, Nero

Poppaea and Nero enter in the early morning light, fondly embracing, and bid farewell to one another with tender caresses.

POPPEA

Si-gnor, si-gnor, deh — non par-ti — re, So-stien — che que-ste
My lord, my lord, pray — do not leave me, Per — mit — these lov-ing

brac-cia Ti cir-con-di-no il col — lo, Co-me le tue bel-lez-ze Cir-con-da-no — il cor mi — o.
arms still to ca-ress and em-brace thee As all your man — ly beau-ties en-close my heart — and en-slave me.

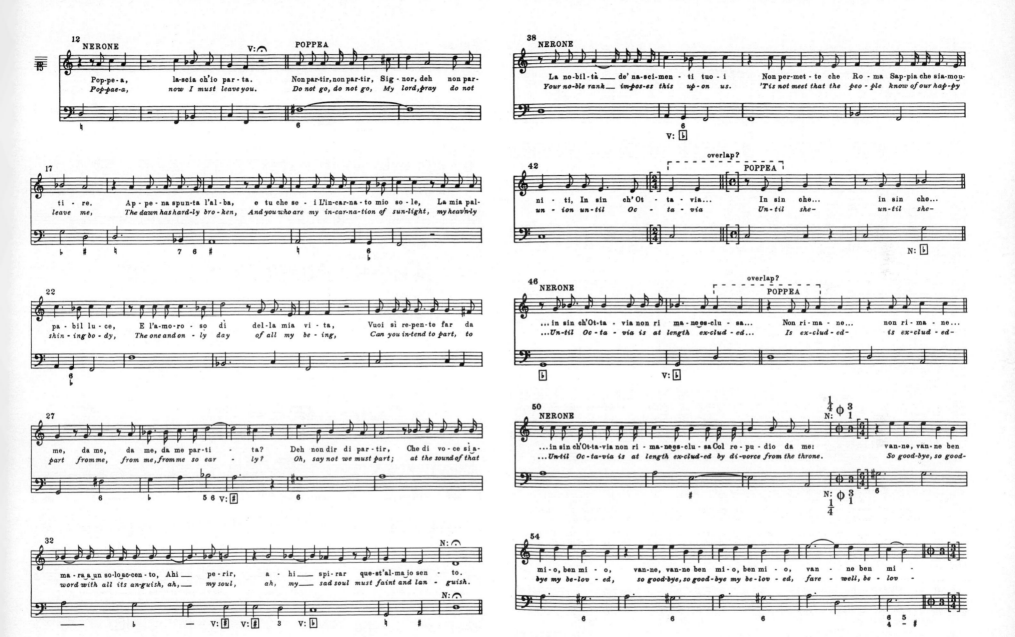

1) N: flat lacking   2) ♭ in both MSS
V: ♯ (by mistake?)
3) Bass bars 136-149 in tenor clef in both N and V, although V mistakenly continues F clef.
4) c″ instead of d″ in both MSS.

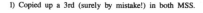
1) Copied up a 3rd (surely by mistake!) in both MSS.

1) When Nerone is sung by a tenor, the d', c#', and d' must also be transposed down an octave.

N: Subito ch'há detto à Dio Poppea ben mio si fá il seguente Ritornello et poi segue scena 4ª
As soon as he has said 'Farewell Poppaea, I leave you', the ensuing Ritornello is performed, and then scene 4.

82. Singet dem Herren ein neues Lied from Symphoniae sacrae II

Heinrich Schütz (1585–1672)

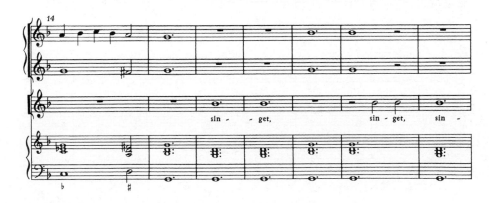

189

191

194

Singet dem Herren ein neues Lied,
singet dem Herren alle Welt.
Singet dem Herrn und lobet seinen Namen.
Prediget einen Tag am andern sein Heil.
Erzählet unter den Heiden seine Ehre,
unter allen Völkern seine Wunder.
Denn der Herr ist groß und hoch zu loben,
wunderbarlich über alle Götter.

O sing unto the Lord a new song:
sing unto the Lord all the earth.
Sing unto the Lord, bless his name;
shew forth his salvation from day to day.
Declare his glory among the heathen,
his wonders among all people.
For the Lord is great, and greatly to be praised:
For he is to be feared above all gods.

Psalm 96: 1–4

83. Saul, was verfolgst du mich?

Schütz

Herausgeber: Günter Graulich
Generalbaßaussetzung: Paul Horn
English text by Derek McCulloch

84. **Armide,** Overture and Act II, Scene 5

Jean-Baptiste Lully (1632–1687)

Ouverture.

*) Den französischen Violinschlüssel transponire ich durchweg auf die zweite Linie. In der zweiten Ausg. fehlen die Mittelstimmen, doch ist sowohl in den Gesang - als Instrumentalsätzen der Bass reicher beziffert. Die zweite Ausg. ist überhaupt nur ein Auszug zu nennen.

+) Die zweite Ausg. setzt für das *t* das Zeichen × und verwendet es öfterer als in der ersten Ausg.

Note: The keyboard reduction here is an editorial addition and not a part of Lully's original score.

SCÈNE V.
Armide, Renaud endormy.

202

Armide. (tenant un dard à la main.)

En _ fin il est en ma puis _ san _ ce. Ce fa_tal en_ne _ mi, ce super_be vain_

queur. La charme du som _ meil le livre à ma ven _ gean_ce; je vais per_

cer son in _ vin_ci _ ble coeur. Par lui tous mes cap_tifs sont sor_tis d'es_cla_

(Armide va pour frapper Renaud et ne

va _ ge; qu'il é _ prouve tou_te ma ra _ ge. Quel trou_ble me sai _ sit?

peut exécuter le dessein qu'elle a de lui ôter la vie.)

qui me fait hé _ si _ ter? qu'est_ce qu'en sa fa _ _veur la pi_tié me veut

di _ re? Frappons ciel! qui peut m'arré _ _ ter? Ache _ vons... je fré _

mis! vengeons_nous... je sou _ pi _ re! Est ce ainsi que je dois me venger aujour_

d'hui! Ma co_lè_re s'é _ teint quand j'appro_che de lui. Plus je le voi, plus ma vengeance est

vaine; mon bras trem_blant se re_fuse á ma hai_ne. Ah! _____ quel_le cru_au_

té de lui ra_vir le jour! A ce jeu_ne hé _ ros tout cè_de sur la ter_re. Qui croi_

rait qu'il fut ne seu_le _ ment pour la guer_re? Il sem_ble e_tre fait pour l'a_

mour. Ne puis_je me ven _ ger á moins qu'il ne pé _ risse? Hé! ne suffit_il

Enfin il est en ma puissance,	Finally he is in my power,
Ce fatal ennemi, ce superbe vainqueur.	this fatal enemy, this superb warrior.
Le charme du sommeille livre à ma vengeance;	The charm of sleep delivers him to my vengeance;
Je vais percer son invincible coeur.	I will pierce his invincible heart.
Par lui tous mes captifs sont sortis d'esclavage;	Through him all my captives have escaped from slavery.
Qu'il éprouve toute ma rage.	Let him feel all my anger.
Quel trouble me saisit? qui me fait hésiter?	What fear grips me? what makes me hesitate?
Qu'est-ce qu'en sa faveur le pitié me veut dire?	What in his favor does pity want to tell me?
Frappons . . . Ciel! qui peut m'arrêter?	Let us strike . . . Heavens! Who can stop me?
Achevons . . . je frémis! vengeons—nous . . . je soupire!	Let us get on with it . . . I tremble! Let us avenge . . . I sigh!
Est-ce ainsi que je dois me venger aujourd'hui?	Is it thus that I must avenge myself today?
Ma colère s'éteint quand j'approche de lui.	My rage is extinguished when I approach him.
Plus je le voi, plus ma vengeance est vaine;	The more I see of him, the more my vengeance is ineffectual.
Mon bras tremblant se refuse à ma haine.	My trembling arm denies my hate.
Ah! quelle cruauté de lui ravir le jour!	Ah! What cruelty, to rob him of the light of day!
A ce jeune héros tout céde sur la terre.	To this young hero everything on earth surrenders.
Qui croirait qu'il fut né seulement pour la guerre?	Who would believe that he was born only for war?
Il semble être fait pour l'Amour.	He seems to be made for love.
Ne puis-je me venger à moins qu'il ne périsse?	Could I not avenge myself unless he dies?
Hé! ne suffit-il pas que l'amour le punisse?	Oh, is it not enough that Love should punish him?
Puisqu'il n'a pu trouver mes yeux assez charmants,	Since he could not find my eyes charming enough,
Qu'il m'aime au moins par mes enchantements.	let him love me at least through my sorcery,
Que, s'il se peut, je le haïsse.	so that, if it's possible, I may hate him.
Venez, venez, seconder mes désirs,	Come, come support my desires,
Démons, transformez-vous en d'aimables zéphirs.	demons; transform yourselves into friendly zephyrs.
Je cède à ce vainqueur, la pitié me surmonte.	I give in to this conqueror; pity overwhelms me.
Cachez ma foiblesse et ma honte	Conceal my weakness and my shame
Dans les plus reculés déserts.	in the most remote desert.
Volez, volez, conduisez-nous au bout de l'univers.	Fly, fly, lead us to the end of the universe.

—Philippe Quinault

85. Giulio Cesare, Act I, Scenes 5–7

George Frideric Handel (1685–1759)

206

207

SCENA VII.

Quartieri nel campo di CESARE con l'urna nel mezzo, ove
sono le ceneri del capo di POMPEO, sopra eminente cumulo di trofei.

CESARE, poi CURIO, che introduce CLEOPATRA e NIRENO.

	Largo.
Violino I.	
Violino II.	
Viola.	
CESARE.	
Bassi.	

SCENA V

CLEOPATRA
Regni Cleopatra; ed al mio seggio intorno
popolo adorator arabo e siro
su questo crin la sacra benda adori:

sù, chi di voi, miei fidi,
ha petto e cor di sollevarmi al trono,

giuri su questa destra eterna fede.

NIRENO
Reina, infausti eventi!

CLEOPATRA
Che fia? ché tardi?

NIRENO
Troncar fé Tolomeo
il capo . . .

CLEOPATRA
Ohimè, di chi?

NIRENO
Del gran Pompeo.

CLEOPATRA
Stelle! Costui che apporta?

NIRENO
Per stabilirsi al soglio
a Cesare mandò fra doni involto . . .

CLEOPATRA
Che gli mandò?

NIRENO
L'esanimato volto.

CLEOPATRA
Sù, partite miei fidi; e tu qui resta.

Alle cesaree tende
son risolta portarmi,
e tu, Nireno, mi servirai di scorta.

SCENE 5

CLEOPATRA
Let Cleopatra reign, and around my throne
Let the adoring peoples of Arabia and Syria
Prostrate themselves before the sacred band
    that engirds my tresses.
Come, let those of you
Who have the mind and heart to raise me upon
    the throne
Swear eternal loyalty on my right hand.

NIRENUS
O Queen, ill-starred events!

CLEOPATRA
What has happened? Why do you delay?

NIRENUS
Ptolemy has
beheaded . . .

CLEOPATRA
O heavens! Whom?

NIRENUS
The great Pompey.

CLEOPATRA
Gods in heaven! What news does this man
    bring?

NIRENUS
To ascertain his throne he sent it,
Among other gifts, wrapped in a veil, to
    Caesar . . .

CLEOPATRA
What did he send?

NIRENUS
The lifeless head.

CLEOPATRA
Go, withdraw, my loyal subjects. You remain
    here.
I have resolved to betake
Myself to Caesar's camp,
And you, Nirenus, shall serve as my escort.

NIRENO
Che dirà Tolomeo?

CLEOPATRA
Non paventar: col guardo,
meglio ch'egli non fece
col capo di Pompeo,
Cesare obligherò.
Invano aspira al trono:
egli è il germano, e la regina io sono.

TOLOMEO
Tu di regnar pretendi,
donna superba e altera?

CLEOPATRA
Io ciò ch'è mio contendo; e la corona
dovuta alla mia fronte
giustamente pretendo.

TOLOMEO
Vanne, e torna omai, folle,
a qual di donna è l'uso:
di scettro invece, a trattar l'ago e il fuso.

CLEOPATRA
Anzi, tu pur, effeminato amante,
va' dell'età sui primi nati albori,
di regno invece, a coltivar gli amori!

    Non disperar, chi sa?
se al regno non l'avrai,
avrai sorte in amor.
    Mirando una beltà
in essa troverai
a consolar un cor.

SCENA VI

ACHILLA
Sire, signor!

TOLOMEO
    Achilla!
Come fu il capo tronco
da Cesare gradito?

NIRENUS
What will Ptolemy say?

CLEOPATRA
Have no fear. With a single look alone
I shall be able to compel Caesar
Better than he did
With the head of Pompey.
In vain he aspires to the throne:
He is my brother, and I am the queen.

PTOLEMY (enters)
You pretend to the throne,
Proud and presumptuous woman?

CLEOPATRA
I contest what is mine, and rightfully
Claim the crown
That belongs to my brow.

PTOLEMY
Get you gone and return, you madwoman,
To your proper place as a woman:
Wield the needle and the distaff instead of the
        sceptre.

CLEOPATRA
It is rather you, effeminate lover,
You, who are still in the dawn of your life,
To go and cultivate your loves instead of the
        kingdom!
    Do not despair: who knows,
    But that you will have the luck in reigning
    That you have in love.
        Gazing on your beauty
    You find in it the way
    To beguile a heart.

SCENE 6

ACHILLA
Sire! Lord!

PTOLEMY
    Achilla!
How did the severed head
Of Pompey please Caesar?

ACHILLA
Sdegnò l'opra.

TOLOMEO
    Che sento?

ACHILLA
T'accusò d'inesperto e troppo ardito.

TOLOMEO
Tant' osa un vil romano?

ACHILLA
    Il mio consiglio
apprendi, o Tolomeo:
verrà Cesare in corte; in tua vendetta
cada costui, come cadé Pompeo.

TOLOMEO
Chi condurrà l'impresa?

ACHILLA
    Io ti prometto
darti estinto il superbo al regio piede,
se di Pompeo la moglie
in premio a me il tuo voler concede.

TOLOMEO
È costei tanto vaga?

ACHILLA
Lega col crine, e col bel volto impiaga.

TOLOMEO
Amico, il tuo consiglio è la mia stella.
Vanne, pensa e poi torna.

Muora Cesare, muora; e il capo altero

sia del mio piè sostegno.
Roma, oppressa da lui, libera vada,
e fermezza al mio regno
sia la morte di lui più che la spada.
    L'empio, sleale, indegno
    vorria rapirmi il regno,
    e disturbar così
    la pace mia.

ACHILLA
He despised the deed.

PTOLEMY
    What do I hear?

ACHILLA
He accused you of misconduct and impudence.

PTOLEMY
A vile Roman has the effrontery?

ACHILLA
    Listen
To my advice, Ptolemy!
Caesar is coming to the court; let him fall victim
To your revenge as Pompey fell.

PTOLEMY
Who will undertake the business?

ACHILLA
    I promise
To lay the haughty corpse at your royal feet,
If in recompense you are willing
To grant me Pompey's wife.

PTOLEMY
Is she so desirable?

ACHILLA
She captivates one with her tresses and pierces
    one's heart with her fair face.

PTOLEMY
Friend, your counsel will be my guiding star:
Go, reflect and return.

Let Caesar die! Let him die! And his proud
    head
Sustain my footing. Let Rome,
Whom he oppresses, regain her freedom,
And his death, more than my sword,
Ascertain my rule.
    The infidel, traitor, villain
    Would rob me of my throne
    And thereby trouble
    My peace of mind.

Ma perda pur la vita,
prima che in me tradita
dall'avido suo cor
la fede sia.

SCENA VII

CESARE
Alma del gran Pompeo,
che al cener suo d'intorno
invisibil t'aggiri,
fur ombra i tuoi trofei,
ombra la tua grandezza, e un'ombra sei.

Così termina alfine il fasto umano.
Ieri chi vivo occupò un mondo in guerra,
oggi risolto in polve un'urna serra.

Tal di ciascuno, ahi lasso,
il principio è di terra e il fine è un sasso.
Misera vita, oh quanto è fral tuo stato!
Ti forma un soffio, e ti distrugge un fiato.

CURIO
Qui nobile donzella
chiede chinarsi al Cesare di Roma.

CESARE
Sen venga pur.

CLEOPATRA
    Tra stuol di damigelle
io servo a Cleopatra.
Lidia m'appello, e sotto il ciel d'Egitto
di nobil sangue nata;
ma Tolomeo mi toglie,
barbaro usurpator, la mia fortuna.

CESARE
(Quanta bellezza un sol sembiante aduna!)
Tolomeo sì tiranno?

CURIO
(Se Cornelia mi sprezza,
oggi a Lidia rivolto
collocherò quest'alma in sì bel volto.)

But rather let him lose his life
Before my confidence
Be betrayed
By his avaricious heart!

SCENE 7

CAESAR
Soul of great Pompey
That hovers invisible
About your ashes,
Your victories were but a shadow,
A shadow was your greatness, and you yourself
    are but a shadow.
To this end comes man's glory.
Yesterday he, who alive, engaged a world in war,
Is today dissolved into ash and is enclosed in an
    urn.
Such, alas, is the fate of everyone,
The beginning is earth, the end a stone.
Wretched life! O, how frail is your condition!
A sigh forms you, a breath destroys you.

CURIO
Here is a noble maiden
Who requests to bow in tribute to Caesar of
    Rome.

CAESAR
Then let her come.

CLEOPATRA
    Among a group of young ladies
I serve Cleopatra.
I am called Lydia and under the skies of Egypt
Was born of noble blood;
But Ptolemy, the villainous brigand,
Has robbed me of my fortune.

CAESAR
(How many beauties are assembled in one face!)
Is Ptolemy such a tyrant?

CURIO
(If Cornelia disdains me,
From today, turning towards Lydia,
My soul will fix itself upon so lovely a face.)

CLEOPATRA
Avanti al tuo cospetto, avanti a Roma,
mesta, afflitta e piangente
chieggio giustizia.

CESARE
    (Oh Dio, come innamora!)
Sfortunata donzella, in breve d'ora
deggio portarmi in corte:
oggi colà stabilirò tua sorte.
(Che bel crin!)

CURIO
    (Che bel sen!)

CLEOPATRA
Signor, i tuoi favori
legan quest'alma.

CESARE
    E la tua chioma i cori.
    Non è sì vago e bello
il fior nel prato,
quant'è vago e gentile
il tuo bel volto.
    D'un fiore il pregio a quello
solo vien dato,
ma tutto un vago aprile
è in te raccolto.

CLEOPATRA
Before your eyes, before Rome,
Mourning, my afflicted, weeping heart
Demands justice.

CAESAR
    (O God! How she inspires me with love!)
Unfortunate maiden, in a few hours
I must go to the court,
And there even today I shall attend to your fate.
(What lovely tresses!)

CURIO
    (What a fair bosom!)

CLEOPATRA
My Lord, your favour
Binds my soul to you.

CAESAR
    And your tresses enchain hearts.
    The flower in the meadow
Is not so charming or so fair
As the loveliness and sweetness
Of your beauteous face.
    It can be compared
Only to the loveliness of a flower,
But all of a fair April
Is joined in you.

86. **Dido and Aeneas,** Act I (excerpt)

Henry Purcell (1659–1695)

ACT I.

Scene. *The Palace. Enter Dido, Belinda, and train.*

Nº 1. SCENA and CHORUS.

No. 2. SONG.

213

215

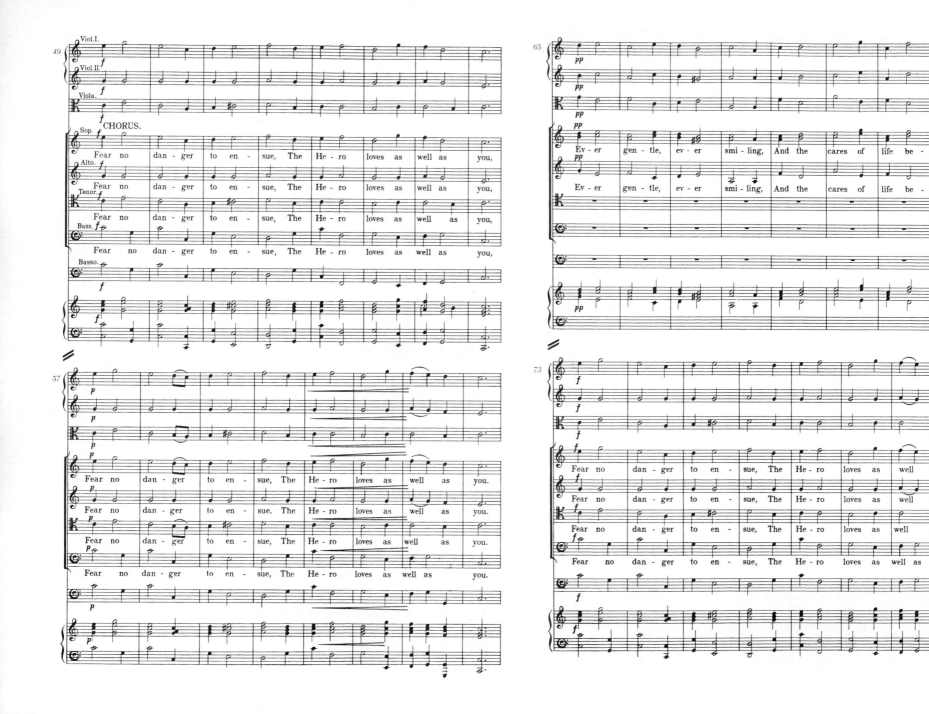

87. The Beggar's Opera (excerpts)

John Gay (1685–1732) and *Johann Christoph Pepusch* (1667–1752)

Air 8. Grim King of the ghosts

POLLY Can Love be con-troul'd by ad-vice? Will Cu-pid our Mo-thers o-bey? Though my heart were as fro-zen as Ice, At his flame 'twould have melt-ed a-way. When he kist me so close-ly he prest, 'Twas so sweet that I must have com-ply'd: So I thought it both saf-est and best To mar-ry, for fear you should chide.

Air 44. Lillibulero

Air 51. Come, sweet lass

MACHEATH The

Tutti   Str.

modes of the Court so com-mon are grown, That a true friend can hard-ly be met;

Friend-ship for in - terest is but a loan, Which they let out for what they can get.

'Tis true, you find Some friends so kind, Who'll give you good coun-sel them -

- selves to de - fend. In sor-row-ful dit - ty, They pro - mise, they pi - ty, But

shift you for mo - ney, from friend to friend.

Tutti

LUCY Come, sweet lass, Let's
Vns.
Str.

Vc.

ba - nish sor - row 'Till to - mor-row; Come, sweet lass, Let's take a chirp-ing Glass.

Wine can clear The va-pours of des - pair; And make us light as air; Then drink, and

1.   2.

ba - nish care.   care.

Str.

220

88. Jephte (excerpt)

Giacomo Carissimi (1605–1674)

Revised and edited by
Janet Beat

HISTORICUS
ALTO

ORGAN

Cum vo-cas-set in proe-li-um fi-li-os Is-ra-el rex fi-li-

o-rum Am-mon, et ver-bis Jeph-te ac-qui-es-ce-re no-lu-is-set,

fac-tus est su-per Jeph-te Spi-ri-tus Do-mi-ni, et pro-

gres-sus ad fi-li-os Am-mon vo-tum vo-vit Do-mi-ni di - cens:

JEPHTE
TENOR

Si tra-di-de-rit Do-mi-nus fi-li-os Am-mon in man-us me-as,

qui-cum-que pri-mus de do-mo me-a oc-cur-re-rit mi-hi,

of-fe-ram il-lum Do-mi-no in ho-lo-cau - stum.

221

CHORUS

SOPRANO I
con Vln. I
Tran-si-vit er-go Jeph-te ad fi-li-os Am - mon,

SOPRANO II
con Vln. II
Tran-si-vit er-go Jeph-te ad fi-li-os Am - mon, ut in spi-ri-tu

SOPRANO III
1)
Tran-si-vit er-go Jeph-te ad fi-li-os Am - mon,

ALTO
Tran-si-vit er-go Jeph-te ad fi-li-os Am - mon,

TENOR
Tran-si-vit er-go Jeph-te ad fi-li-os Am - mon,

BASS
Tran-si-vit er-go Jeph-te ad fi-li-os Am - mon, ut in

♩=100
mf   f
22   6

for - ti et vir - tu - te, et vir - tu - te_ Do - mi - ni pug-

ut in spi - ri-tu for - ti et vir - tu - te_ Do - mi - ni   pug-

pug - na - ret,
2)
spi - ri-tu for - ti et vir - tu - te, et vir - tu - te_ Do - mi - ni pug-

26

1) Bar 23, Soprano III. ♩. ♪ in A
2) Bar 27, Bass. ♩♪ in A

con Vln. I
pug - na - ret con - tra e - os, pug-na - ret,   pug-

na - ret,   con Vln.II   pug - na - ret,   pug-

con Vln. II
na - ret,   pug - na - ret con - tra e - os,   pug-

pug - na - ret, pug-na - ret con - tra e - os,_ pug - na - ret,

pug - na - ret con - tra e - os, pug - na - ret,   pug-

na - ret,   pug - na - ret,   pug - na - ret,

28   4 3   4 3 [sic]

na-ret con-tra e - os,   pug-na-ret con-tra e - os.

na-ret con-tra e - os,   pug - na-ret con - tra e - os, con-tra e - os.

na-ret con-tra e - os,   pug-na-ret con - tra e - os, con-tra e - os.

pug - na - ret, pug-na-ret con-tra e - os, con-tra e - os.

na-ret con-tra e - os, pug - na - ret,   pug - na-ret con-tra e - os.

pug - na - ret,   pug - na-ret con-tra e - os, con-tra e - os.

30   4 3   4 3   4 3

222

3) Bar 35, Continuo in A reads [music notation] but Charpentier has written beneath it the version here given with the legend 'Caris.' (? Carissimi).

4) Bar 37, Continuo in A reads [music notation] but again Charpentier has written beneath it the version here given with the same legend.

5) Bar 52, Bass in A reads [music notation]

pug-nat con-tra vos,   et pug-nat con-tra vos, _____ et

53

pug-nat con-tra vos, et pug - - nat con - tra vos.

56

CHORUS

S I   con Vln.I

Fu - gi-te, fu - gi-te, ce-di-te, ce - di - te,   im - pi - i, fu - gi - te, fu - gi - te,

S II   7)   con Vln.II

Fu - gi-te, fu - gi-te, ce-di-te, ce - di - te,   im - pi - i, fu - gi - te, fu - gi - te,

S III   6)

Fu - gi-te, fu - gi-te, ce-di-te, ce - di - te,   im - pi - i, fu - gi - te, fu - gi - te,

A

Fu - gi - te, fu - gi - te,

T

Fu - gi - te, fu - gi - te,

B

Fu - gi - te, fu - gi - te,

♩ = 96

f

59

6) Bar 59, Soprano III.   in A

7) Bar 60, Soprano II.
    Bar 61, Tenor.   in A

ce-di-te, ce-di-te, im-pi-i,   senza Vln.II   et in fu-ro-re gla-di-i dis-si-

ce-di-te, ce-di-te, im-pi-i,   8)   cor-ru - i - te,

ce-di-te, ce-di-te, im-pi-i,   cor-ru - i - te,

ce-di-te, ce-di-te, im-pi-i,   7)

ce-di-te, ce-di-te, im-pi-i,

ce-di-te, ce-di-te, im-pi-i,

61   4 3   #

                                     con Vln.I

pa-mi-ni,   fu-gi-te, fu-gi-te, ce-di-te, ce-di-te,
                             con Vln.II

fu-gi-te, fu-gi-te, ce-di-te, ce-di-te,

fu-gi-te, fu-gi-te, ce-di-te, ce-di-te,

fu-gi-te, fu-gi-te, ce-di-te,ce-di-te,im-pi-i, fu-gi-te, fu-gi-te, ce-di-te, ce-di-te,

fu-gi-te,fu-gi-te, ce-di-te,ce-di-te,im-pi-i, fu-gi-te, fu-gi-te, ce-di-te, ce-di-te,

fu-gi-te,fu-gi-te, ce-di-te,ce-di-te,im-pi-i, fu-gi-te, fu-gi-te, ce-di-te, ce-di-te,

64   4 3   4 3

8) Bar 62, Soprano III. ♪♪ in A

* Bars 70-71. There is much to be said for taking this organ bass an octave higher.

* Bars 78-88. There is much to be said for taking this organ bass an octave higher.

225

HISTORICUS

Cum vocasset in proelium filios Israel rex filiorum Ammon, et verbis Jephte acquiescere noluisset, factus est super Jephte Spiritus Domini, et progressus ad filios Ammon votum vovit Domini dicens:

When the king of the children of Ammon made war against the children of Israel, and hearkened not unto the words of Jephthah, then there came upon Jephthah the Spirit of the Lord, and he went up against the children of Ammon and vowed unto the Lord, saying:

JEPHTE

Si tradiderit Dominus filios Ammon in manus meas, quicumque primus de domo mea occurrerit mihi, offeram illum Domino in holocaustum.

If thou shalt indeed deliver the children of Ammon into my hands, whatsoever first cometh forth of the doors of my house to meet me, I will offer to the Lord for a burnt offering.

CHORUS

Transivit ergo Jephte ad filios Ammon, ut in spiritu forti et virtute Domini pugnaret contra eos.

Then Jephthah passed over to the children of Ammon, and he fought in the spirit and the strength of God against them.

DUET

Et clangebant tubae, et personabant tympana, et proelium commissum est adversus Ammon.

And the trumpets sounded, and the drums were beaten, when battle was joined against the children of Ammon.

BASS SOLO

Fugite, cedite, impii, perite gentes, occumbite in gladio; Dominus exercituum in proelium surrexit, et pugnat contra vos.

Flee from us, yield to us, impious ones, give away, ye heathen, and fall before our mighty sword; for the God of Israel is risen up to battle and fights against our foes.

CHORUS

Fugite, cedite, impii, corruite, et in furore gladii dissipamini.

Flee from us, yield to us, impious ones, we scatter you, and with our keen and glittering swords we hew you down.

HISTORICUS

Et percussit Jephte viginti civitates Ammon plaga magna nimis.

Jephthah therefore smote them, and took from them twenty cities, and there was a grievous slaughter.

TRIO

Et ululantes filii Ammon, facti sunt coram filiis Israel humiliati.

And he subdued the children of Ammon, for the Lord delivered them to the children of Israel.

HISTORICUS

Cum autem victor Jephte in domum suam reverteretur, occurrens ei unigenita filia sua cum tympanis et choris praecinebat:

And Jephthah came to Mispeh unto his house when he returned, and behold, there came forth his only daughter to meet him with timbrels and with dances, and she sang thus:

FILIA

Incipite in tympanis et psallite in cymbalis. Hymnum cantemus Domino, et modulemur canticum. Laudemus regem coelitum, laudemus belli principem, qui filiorum Israel victorem ducem reddidit.

Come, strike the merry timbrels and sound the joyful cymbals. Let us sing praises unto the Lord, and let us magnify his name, yea, let us praise the God of heaven and magnify the mighty King who doth restore the conquering leader of the children of Israel.

228

DUET

Hymnum cantemus Domino, et modulemur canticum, qui dedit nobis gloriam et Israel victoriam.

FILIA

Cantate mecum Domino, cantate omnes populi, laudate belli principem, qui nobis dedit gloriam et Israel victoriam.

Sing unto the Lord, and offer hymns to him who giveth us the glory and Israel the victory.

Sing to the Lord with me, sing praises, all ye peoples, to the mighty King who giveth us the glory and Israel the victory.

89. Zadok the Priest

Handel

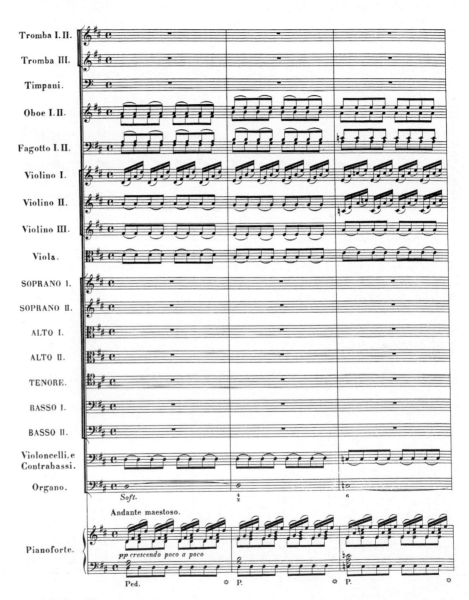

Note: The pianoforte part in this score is for rehearsal purposes only and is not part of Handel's original score.

231

235

237

90. Jesu, der du meine Seele, BWV 78 (excerpts)

Johann Sebastian Bach (1685–1750)

245

Da Capo

250

5. Recitativo

252

7. Choral

1. Chorus: Jesu, der du meine Seele

| Jesu, der du meine Seele hast durch deinen bittern Tod | Jesus, thou who my soul has through your bitter death |

aus des Teufels finstrer Höhle und der schweren Seelennoth

from the devil's dark hell and the severe need of the soul

kräftiglich herausgerissen,

powerfully lifted out

und mich Solches lassen wissen

and gave this known to me

durch dein angenehmes Wort:

through your comforting word:

sei doch jetzt, o Gott, mein Hort!

Be thou now, o God, my protection!

2. Aria (Duet): Wir eilen

Wir eilen mit schwachen, doch emsigen Schritten,
o Jesu, o Meister, zu helfen zu dir.
Du suchest die Kranken und Irrenden treulich.
Ach! höre, wie wir die Stimme erheben,
um Hülfe zu bitten!
Es sei uns dein gnädiges Antlitz erfreulich!

We hasten with weak, yet eager steps,
oh Jesus, oh Master, for help toward thee.
You visit the sick and wayward faithfully.
Ah! hear, how we our voices lift
for help to ask
May us your graceful countenance brighten!

5. Recitative: Die Wunden

Die Wunden, Nägel, Kron' und Grab,
die Schläge, so man dort dem Heiland gab,
sind ihm nunmerhro Siegeszeichen,
und können mir erneute Kräfte reichen.
Wenn ein erschreckliches Gericht
den Fluch für die Verdammten spricht:
so kehrst du ihm in Segen.
Mich kann kein Schmerz und keine Pein bewegen,
weil sie mein Heiland kennt,
und da dein Herz für mich in Liebe brennt,
so lege ich hinwieder das meine vor dir nieder.
Dies, mein Herz, mit Leid vermenget,
so dein theures Blut besprenget,
so am Kreuz vergossen ist,
geb' ich dir, Herr Jesu Christ.

The wounds, nails, crown, and grave,
the blows, that were given the Saviour there
are to him now signs of victory
and can to me renewed powers give.
If a terrible court
the curse of the damned pronounces:
so shall you reverse it [the curse] into a blessing.
No suffering and no pain can move me.

Because my Saviour knows them [too],
and because your heart for me in love burns,
thus I present back to you my heart.
This, my heart, with suffering heaped,
as your dear blood flows,
as it on the cross poured out,
so give I myself to you, Lord Jesus Christ.

6. Aria: Nun du wirst mein Gewissen stillen

Nun du wirst mein Gewissen stillen,
So wider mich um Rache schreit,

Ja, deine Treue wird's erfüllen,
Weil mir dein Wort die Hoffnung beut.
Wenn Christen an dich glauben,
Wird sie kein Feind in Ewigkeit
Aus deinen Händen rauben.

7. Chorale: Herr, ich glaube

Herr, ich glaube, hilf mir Schwachen,
laß mich ja verzagen nicht;
du, du kannst mich stärker machen,
wenn mich Sünd und Tod anficht.
Deiner Güte will ich trauen,
bis ich fröhlich werde schauen
dich, Herr Jesu, nach dem Streit
in der süßen Ewigkeit.

Now you shall my conscience calm,
Which, against my will, for vengeance screams
    out,
Yes, your faithfulness will fill it,
Because to me your word offers hope.
When Christians in you believe,
No enemy in all eternity
will steal them from your hands.

Lord, I believe, help me, a weakling,
let me falter not;
thou, thou canst me stronger make,
when sin and death assault me.
Your goodness will I trust,
until I gladly see
you, Lord Jesus, after the battle
in sweet eternity

91. Concerto grosso in F Major, Op. 6, No. 2
Arcangelo Corelli (1653–1713)

256

257

261

92. **Concerto in A minor,** Op. 3, No. 8, first movement
Antonio Vivaldi (1678–1741)

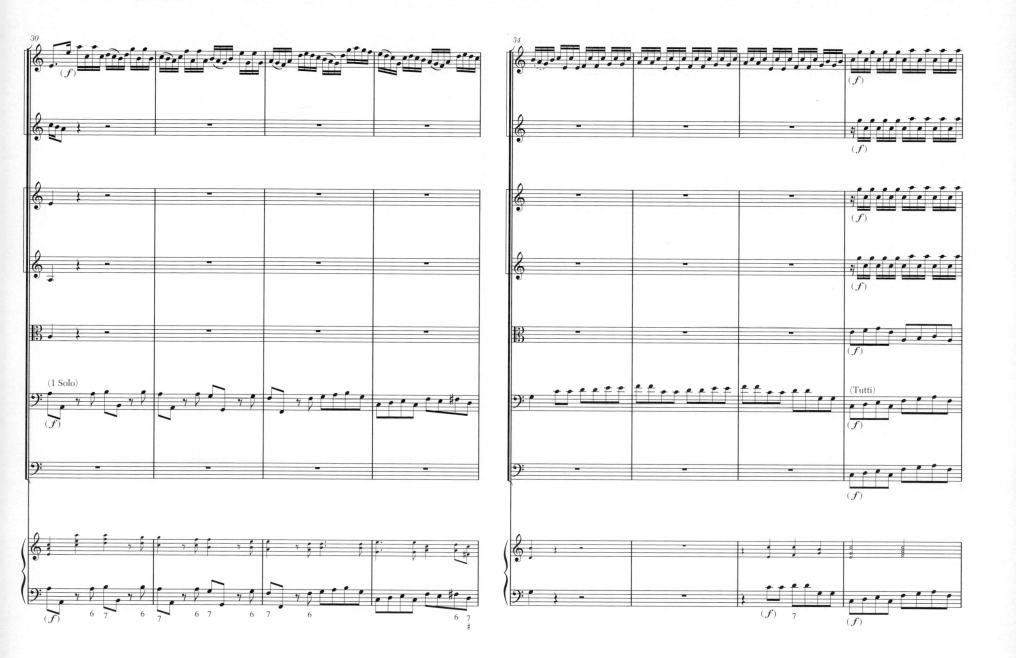

273

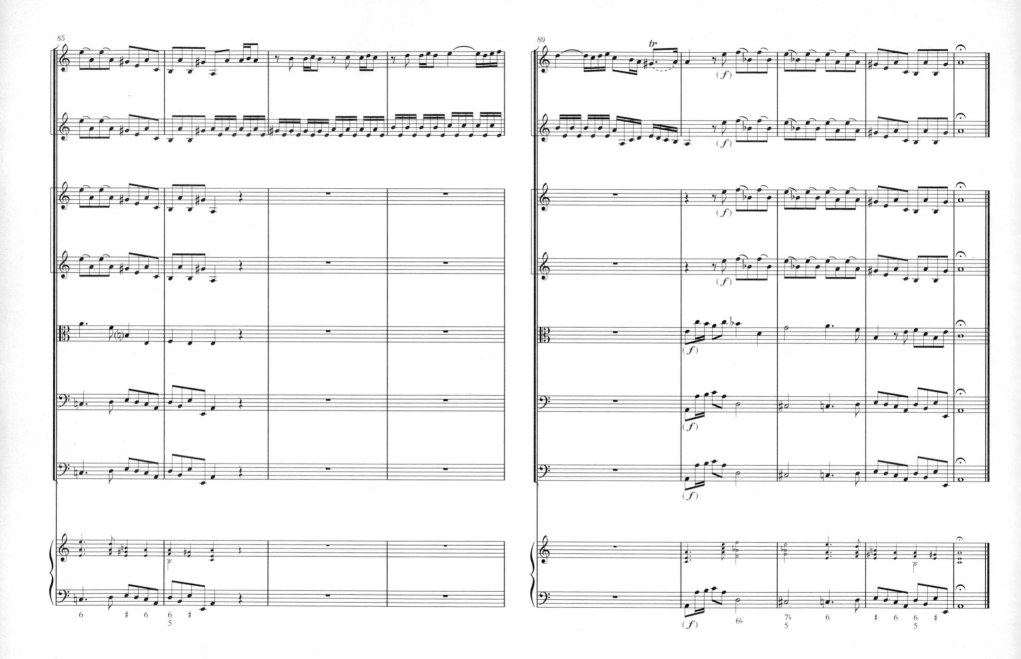

93. Pièces de clavecin (1707): Courante and Gigue

Elisabeth Jacquet de la Guerre (1665–1729)

Courante

Gigue

Double

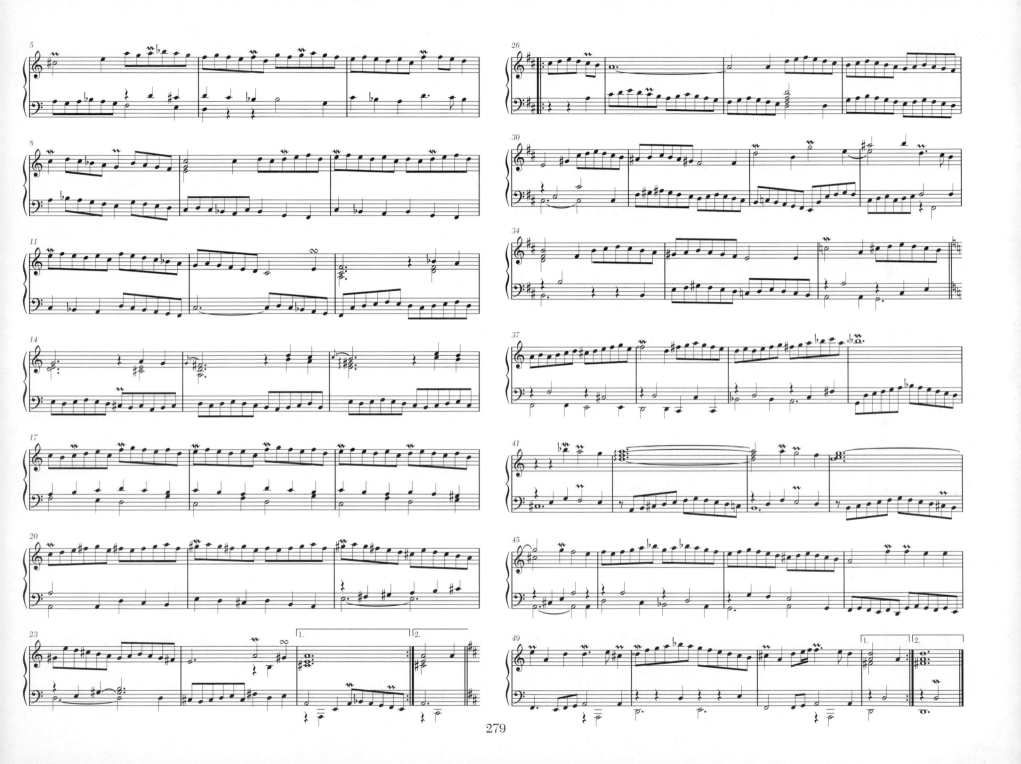

279

2me Gigue

94. Musicalische Vorstellung einiger Biblischer Historien, in 6 Sonaten auff dem Claviere zu spielen, Sonata 1: Il Combattimento trà David e Goliath (excerpts)

Johann Kuhnau (1660–1722)

Il tremore degl'Israliti alla comparsa del Gigante, e la loro preghiera fatta a Dio.

Il Coraggio di David, ed il di lui ardore di rintuzzar l'orgoglio del nemico spaventevole, colla sua confidenza messa nell'ajuto di Dio.

Il combattere frà l'uno e l'altro e la loro contesa.

vien tirata la selce colla
frombola nella fronte del Gigante.

casca Goliath.

La fuga de' Filistei, che vengono perseqvitati ed amozzati dagl' Israeliti.

282

Il tremore degli israeliti alla comparsa del
  gigante, e la loro preghiera fatta a Dio.
Il coraggio di David, ed il di lui ardore di
  rintuzzar l'orgoglio del nemico spaventevole,
  colla sua confidenza messa nell'ajuto di Dio

Il combattere frà l'uno e l'altro e la loro contesa,

vien tirata la selce colla frombola nella fronte
  del Gigante
casca Goliath.
La fuga de' Filistei, che vengono persequitati ed
  amozzati dagl'Israeliti.

The trembling of the Israelites at the sight of
  the giant, and their prayer to God.
The courage of David, and his zeal to break
  the pride of the horrible enemy, and his
  confidence in placing himself into the hands
  of God.
The combat between the two and their
  exchange of words,
in which the slung stone strikes the giant in the
  forehead and
Goliath falls.
The flight of the Philistines, pursued and
  slaughtered by the Israelites.

95. Les élémens: first movement, "Le cahos"
Jean-Féry Rebel (1661–1747)

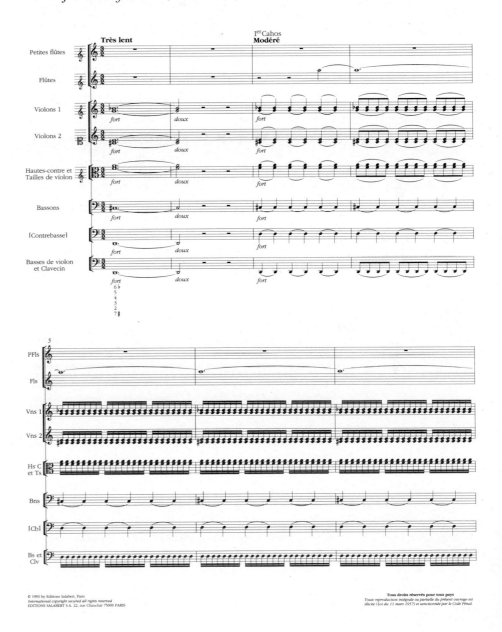

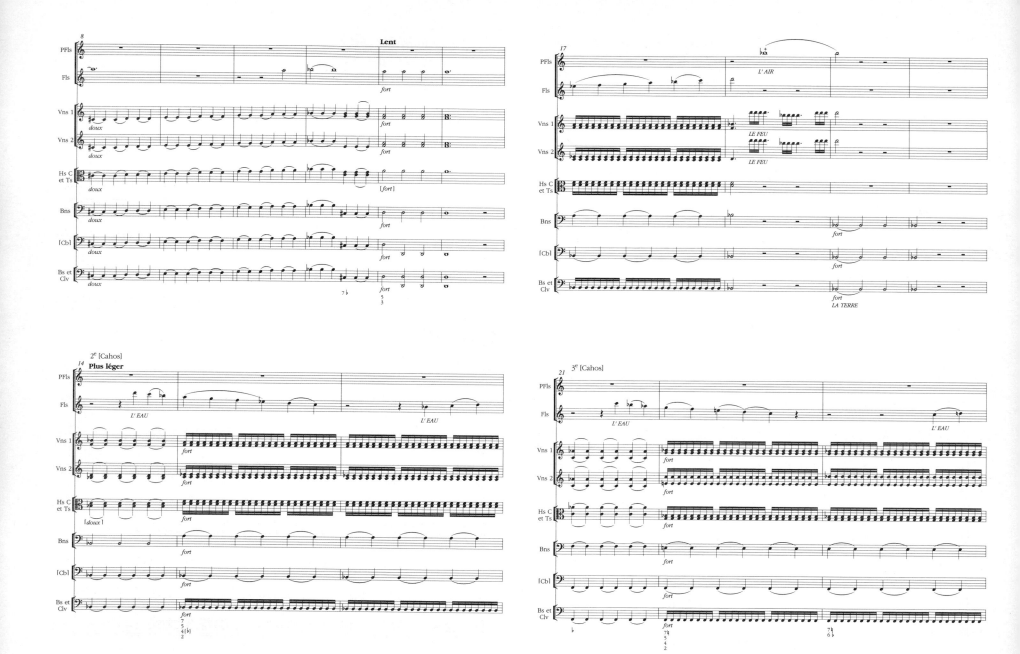

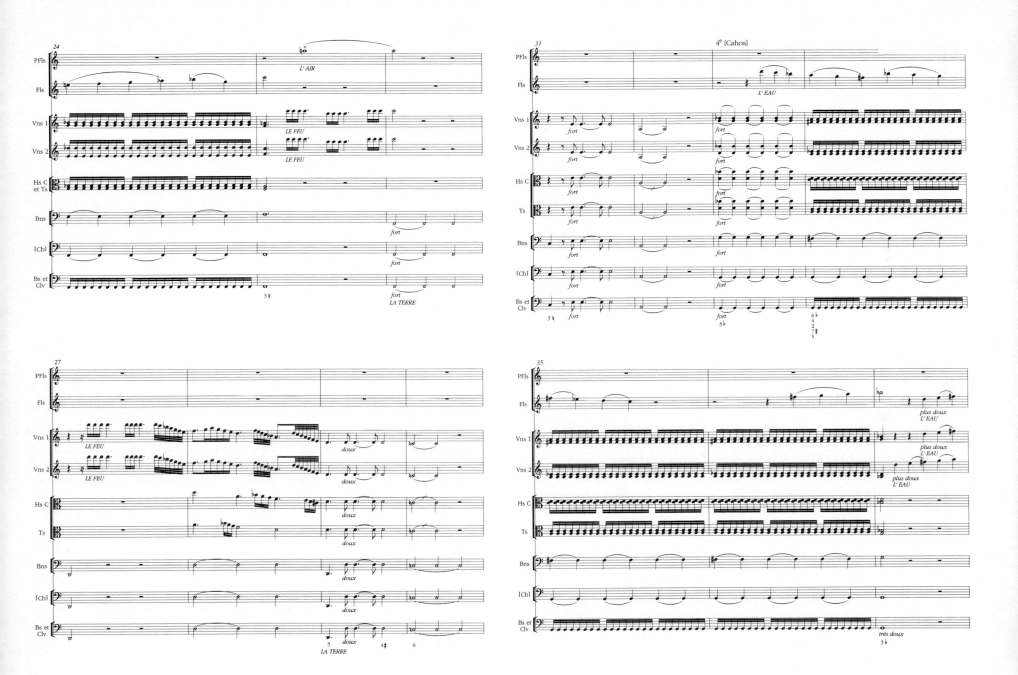

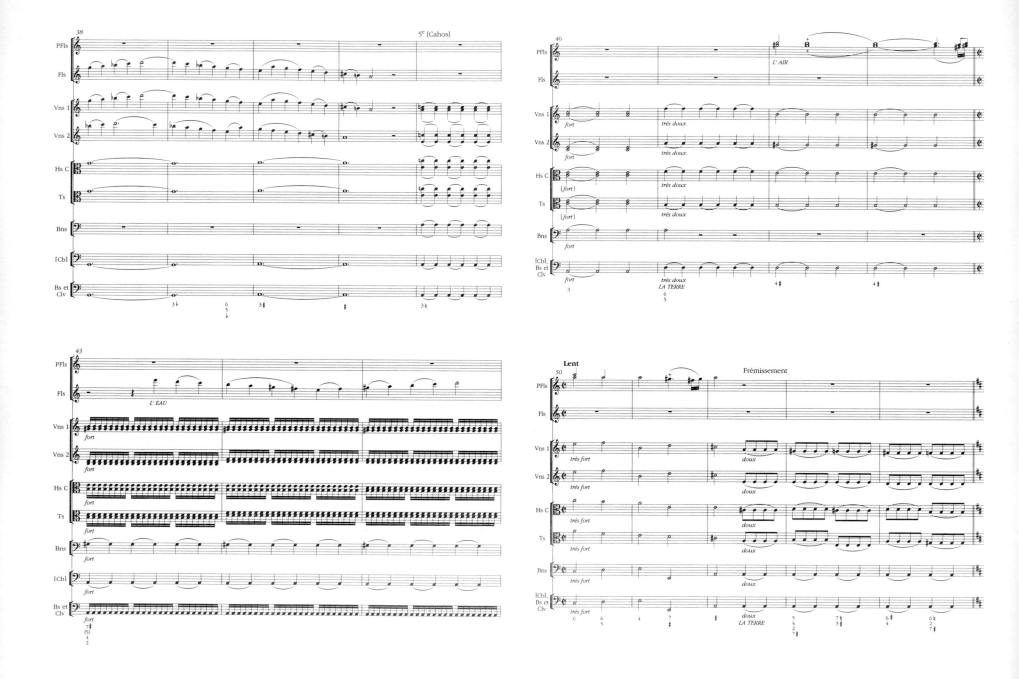

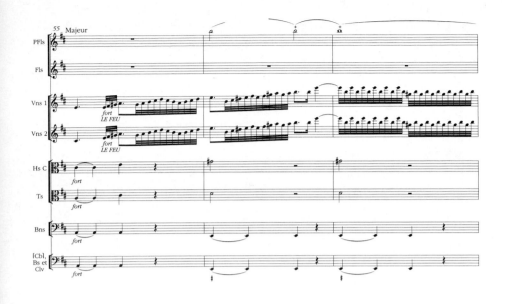

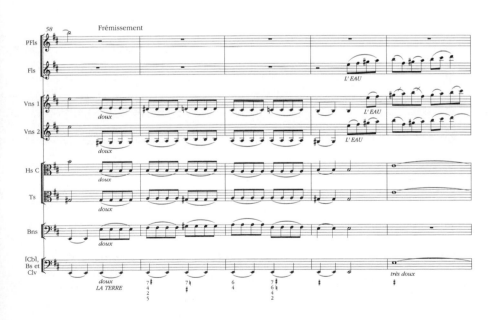

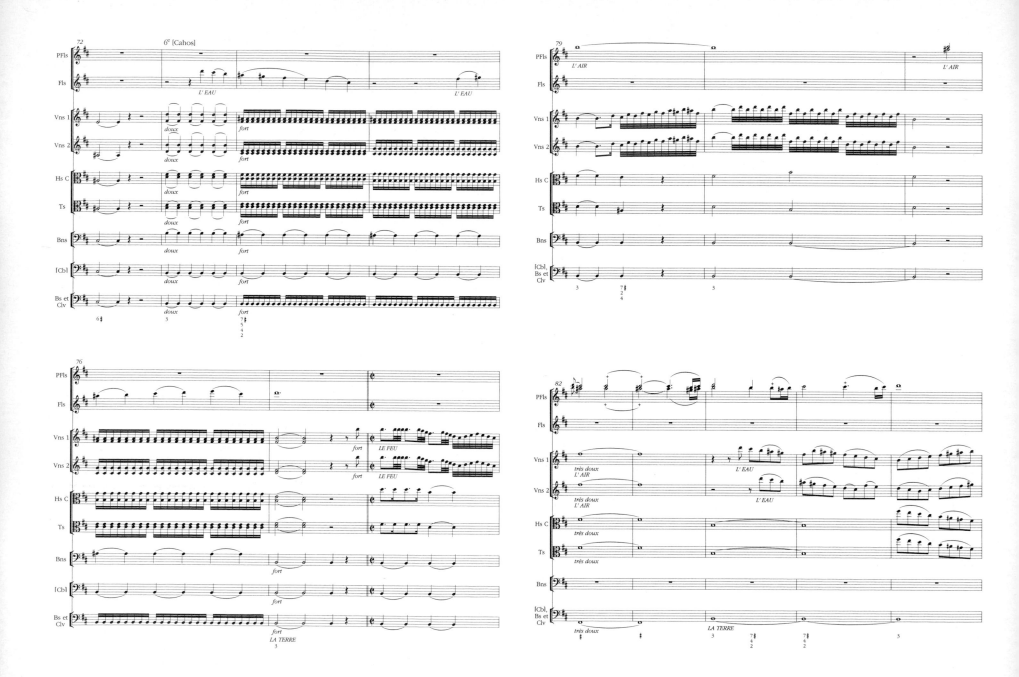

289

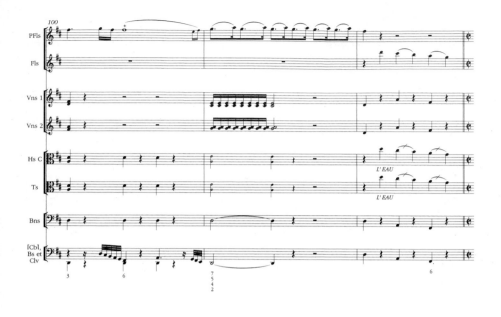

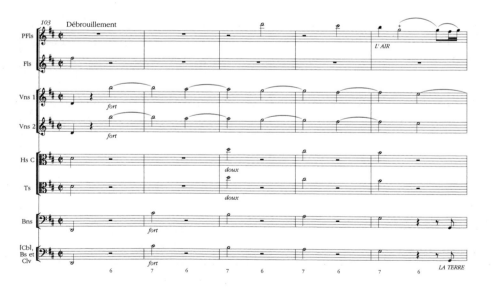

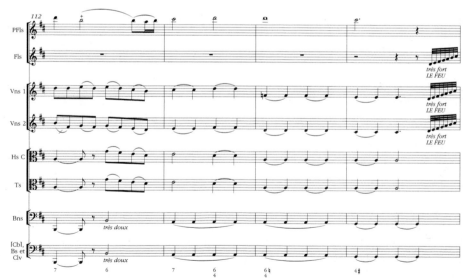

290

291

96. **Toccata IX** from **Il Secondo Libro di Toccate**

Girolamo Frescobaldi (1583–1643)

Non senza fatiga si giunge al fine

97. Praeludium in G minor, BuxWV 149

Dietrich Buxtehude (1637–1707)

98. The Well-Tempered Clavier, Book I (excerpts)

J. S. Bach

Prelude and Fugue No. 1 in C Major

Prelude and Fugue No. 4 in C♯ minor

99. Chorale prelude on the **Magnificat peregrini toni**
Johann Pachelbel (1652–1706)

100. Chorale prelude on **Meine Seele erhebt den Herren, BWV 645**, from **Sechs Choräle von verschiedener Art** (the "Schübler" chorales)

J. S. Bach

101. **Aria mit dreißig Veränderungen** ("Goldberg" Variations), Aria and variations 1–7

J. S. Bach

ARIA.

Variatio 2. a 1 Clav.

Variatio 3. Canone all' Unisono. a 1 Clav.

Variatio 6. Canone alla Seconda. a 1 Clav.

Variatio 7. a 1 ovvero 2 Clav.

CREDITS

1. Epitaph of Seikilos. Reprinted with permission of the publisher from Thomas J. Mathiesen, *Apollo's Lyre: Greek Music and Music Theory in Antiquity and the Middle Ages* (Lincoln: The University of Nebraska Press). © 1999 by the University of Nebraska Press.

2. Mass for Easter Sunday. English translation reprinted by permission from Richard H. Hoppin (ed.), *Anthology of Medieval Music*. Copyright 1978 by W. W. Norton & Company, Inc.

3. Vespers on Easter Sunday: Antiphon *Angelus autem Domini* and Psalm 109 *Dixit Dominus*. English translation of "Dixit Dominus" from *Marianna von Martines: Dixit Dominus*, edited by Irving Godt, Recent Researches in the Music of the Classical Era, vol. 48 (Madison, WI: A-R Editions, Inc., 1977).

4. Hymn Pange lingua gloriosi.

5. Hildegard von Bingen, *Ordo Virtutum*, scene 4 (excerpt). © Hildegard Publishing Company. Reprinted with permission of the publisher.

6. Beatriz de Dia, *A chantar*. Reprinted with permission of the author from Hendrik van der Werf, *The Extant Troubadour Melodies* (Rochester, NY: Author, 1984).

7. *A Santa Maria dadas*, from the *Cantigas de Santa Maria*, Cantiga 140. Reprinted with permission of the publisher from Martin Cunningham, ed., Alfonso X el Sabio, *Cantigas de Loor* (Dublin: University College Dublin Press, 2000).

8. Walther von der Vogelweide, *Palästinalied*.

9. Kyrie *Cunctipotens genitor deus*. Codex Calixtinus, Cathedral of Santiago da Compostela, f. 190. Reprinted with permission from Heinrich Husmann, ed., *Medieval Polyphony: Das Musikwerk*, vol. 9 (Cologne: Arno Volk Verlag, 1962). © 2003 by Laaber-Verlag, Laaber, Germany. English translation © Jeremy Yudkin, used by permission.

10. Léonin (?), Organum *Haec dies*, W1, f. 31. Reprinted with permission from Heinrich Husmann, ed., *Die mittelalterliche Mehrstimmigkeit: Das Musikwerk*, vol. 9 (Cologne: Arno Volk-Verlag, n.d. [1960?]). © 2003 by Laaber-Verlag, Laaber, Germany.

11. Clausula *In saeculum*, W2, f. 72r. Reprinted with permission from Heinrich Husmann, ed., *Die mittelalterliche Mehrstimmigkeit: Das Musikwerk*, vol. 9 (Cologne: Arno Volk-Verlag, n.d. [1960?]). © 2003 by Laaber-Verlag, Laaber, Germany.

12. Motet *Lonc tens ai mon cuer / In seculum*. Reprinted with permission from Hans Tischler, ed., *The Montpellier Codex*, Part 3: *Fascicles 6, 7, and 8*, Recent Researches in the Music of the Middle Ages and Early Renaissance, vol. 6-7 (Madison, WI: A-R Editions, Inc., 1978).

13. Motet *Huic main / Haec dies*. Reprinted with permission from Hans Tischler, ed., *The Montpellier Codex*, Part 3: *Fascicles 6, 7, and 8*, Recent Researches in the Music of the Middle Ages and Early Renaissance, vol. 6–7 (Madison, WI: A-R Editions, Inc., 1978).

14. Motet *A Paris / On parole / Frese nouvelle*. Reprinted with permission from Hans Tischler, ed., *The Montpellier Codex*, Part 3: *Fascicles 6, 7, and 8*, Recent Researches in the Music of the Middle Ages and Early Renaissance, vol. 6–7 (Madison, WI: A-R Editions, Inc., 1978). English translation by Michael J. Freeman from *The European Musical Heritage, 800–1750* [compiled by] Sarah Fuller; consulting editor in music, Allan W. Schindler. 1/e. NY: Knopf, © 1987. By permission of The McGraw-Hill Companies.

15. Conductus *Flos ut rosa floruit*. Reprinted from Jeremy Yudkin, *Music in Medieval Europe*, © 1989, by permission of Pearson Education, Inc., Upper Saddle River, NJ.

16. Philippe de Vitry (?), *Garrit Gallus / In nova fert / Neuma*. English translation reprinted by permission from Richard H. Hoppin (ed.), *Anthology of Medieval Music*. Copyright 1978 by W. W. Norton & Company, Inc.

17. Guillaume de Machaut, *La Messe de Nostre Dame* (Kyrie). Reprinted with permission from Leo Schrade, ed., Guillaume de Machaut, *Oeuvres complètes*, vol. 3: *La Messe de Nostre-Dame* (Monaco: Editions de l'Oiseau-Lyre, 1977).

18. Machaut, *Je puis trop bien ma dame comparer*. Reprinted with permission from Leo Schrade, ed., Guillaume de Machaut, *Oeuvres complètes*, vol. 4: *Les Ballades, Les Virelais* (Monaco: Editions de l'Oiseau-Lyre, 1977). English translation reprinted by permission of the publisher from *The Historical Anthology of Music—Volume I: Oriental, Medieval, and Rennaissance Music*, edited by Archibald T. Davidson and Willi Apel (Cambridge, MA: Harvard University Press), Copyright © 1946, 1949 by the President and Fellows of Harvard College.

19. Machaut, *Douce dame jolie*. Reprinted with permission from Leo Schrade, ed., Guillaume de Machaut, *Oeuvres complètes*, vol. 4: *Les Ballades, Les Virelais* (Monaco: Editions de l'Oiseau-Lyre, 1977). English translation by permission of Hyperion Records Ltd. from *The Mirror of Narcissus*.

20. Machaut, *Ma fin est mon commencement*.

21. Baude Cordier, *Tout par compas*. Reprinted with permission from Gordon K. Greene, ed., *French Secular Music: Manscript Chantilly, Musée Condé 564: Polyphonic Music of the Fourteenth Century*, vol. 18 (Monaco: Editions de l'Oiseau-Lyre, c1981–c1982). English translation courtesy of New Albion Records from *Ars Magis Subtiliter: Secular Music of the Chantilly Codex*.

22. Francesco Landini, *Ecco la primavera*. Reprinted with permission from Leo Schrade, ed., *Francesco Landini, Complete Works*, vol. 1: *Two-Part Ballate* (Monaco: Editions de l'Oiseau-Lyre, 1982). English translation from *I am Music: Works by Franceso Landini*, Move Records, Carlton, South Australia, 1997.

23. Jacopo da Bologna, *Non al suo amante*. English translation from *The European Musical Heritage, 800–1750* [compiled by] Sarah Fuller; consulting editor in music, Allan W. Schindler. 1/e. NY: Knopf, © 1987. By permission of The McGraw-Hill Companies.

24. Lorenzo da Firenze, *A poste messe*. Reprinted with permission of the American Institute of Musicology, Inc., Middleton, Wisc. from Nino Pirrotta, ed., *The Music of Fourteenth-Century Italy*, vol. 3: Corpus mensurabilis musicae, 8 (American Institute of Musicology, 1962). English translation courtesy of Vanguard Classics, © 1974.

25. Johannes Ciconia, *Doctorum principem / Melodia suavissima / Vir mitis*. Reprinted with permission from Margaret Bent and Anne Hallmark, eds., *The Works of Johannes Ciconia* (Monaco: Editions de l'Oiseau-Lyre, 1982).

26. Anonymous, *Sumer is icumen in*. Reprinted with the permission of the publisher from Frank Ll. Harrsion and E.J. Dobson, eds., *Medieval English Songs* (N.Y.: Cambridge University Press, 1979). English translation MEB.

27. Anonymous, *Edi be thu, heven-queene*. Reprinted with the permission of the publisher from Frank Ll. Harrsion and E.J. Dobson, eds., *Medieval English Songs* (N.Y.: Cambridge University Press, 1979).

28. *La quinte estampie real*. Paris, BN fond français 844 ("Chansonnier du Roi"). Published in Timothy McGee, ed., *Medieval Instrumental Dances* (Bloomington: Indiana University Press, 1989).

29. John Dunstable, *Quam pulchra es*.

30. Guillaume Du Fay, *Flos florum*. Reprinted with permission of the American Institute of Musicology, Inc., Middleton, Wisc. from Heinrich Besseler, ed., Guillaume Du Fay, *Opera omnia* vol. 1: *Motetti* (Rome: American Institute of Musicology, 1966). English translation by Hans Heimler, © 1975 Deutsche Grammophon GmbH, from LP Archiv Produktion 2533 291, by kind permission of Deutsche Grammophon, Hamburg, Germany.

31. Du Fay, *Conditor alme siderum*.

32. Du Fay, *Nuper rosarum flores*. English translation from *Norton Anthology of Western Music*, Vol. 1, edited by Claude V. Palisca.

33. Josquin des Prez, *Ave Maria . . . virgo serena*. English translation MEB.

34. Du Fay, Ballade, *Se la face ay pale*. English translation MEB.

35. Du Fay, Kyrie and Gloria from Mass *Se la face ay pale*. Reprinted with permission of the American Institute of Musicology, Inc., Middleton, Wisc. from Heinrich Besseler, ed. (rev. David Fallows), Guillaume Du Fay, *Opera omnia*, vol. 6 (American Institute of Musicology, Neuhausen-Stuttgart: Hänssler-Verlag, 1995).

36. Johannes Ockeghem, Kyrie from *Missa prolationum*.

37. Anonymous (Busnois?), *Fortuna desperata*. Reprinted from Reinhard Strohm, *The Rise of European Music* (Cambridge: Cambridge University Press, 1993) by permission of the publisher and of Reinhard Strohm, Professor of Music, Oxford University. English translation from *Fortuna Desperata: Thirty-Six Settings of an Italian Song*, edited by Honey Meconi, Recent Researches in the Music of the Middle Ages and Early Renaissance, vol. 37 (Madison, WI: A-R Editions, Inc., 2001).

38. Josquin, *Missa Fortuna desperata* (Kyrie and Agnus Dei). Edition prepared by A-R Editions, Inc. All rights reserved.

39. Josquin, Kyrie from *Missa pange lingua*.

40. Josquin or Pierre de la Rue, *Absalon, fili mi*. English translation MEB.

41. Du Fay, Rondeau *Adieu ces bons vins de Lannoys*. English translation by Keith Anderson from *Dufay Chansons*, courtesy of Naxos of America.

42. Hayne van Ghizighem, *De tous biens plaine*. Reprinted with permission of the American Institute of Musicology, Inc., Middleton, Wisc. from Barton Hudson, ed., Hayne van Ghizighem, *Opera omnia*: Corpus mensurabilis musicae, 74 (Neuhausen-Stuttgart: American Institute of Musicology, 1977). English translation from *De tous biens plaine: Twenty-Eight Settings of Hayne van Ghizeghern's Chanson*, edited by Cynthia J. Cyrus, Recent Researches in the Music of the Middle Ages and Early Renaissance, vol. 36 (Madison, WI: A-R Editions, Inc., 2001).

43. Heinrich Isaac, *Helas, que devera mon coeur*. Reprinted with permission of the publisher from Howard Mayer Brown, ed., *A Florentine Chansonnier from the Time of Lorenzo the Magnificent: Florence, Biblioteca nazionale centrale, MS Banco rari 229* (Chicago: University of Chicago Press, © 1983). English translation by permission of Bernard Thomas (Bradford, U.K.: London Pro Musica).

44. Marchetto Cara, *Hor venduto ho la speranza*. Reprinted from Bevenuto Disertori, ed., *Le frottole per canto e liuto intabulate da Frqanciscus Bossinensis* (Milan: Ricordi, 1964). English translation from *Renaissance Music from the Courts of Mantua & Ferrara, circa 1500* (Musical Heritage Society, 513401K), translation by Peggy Forsyth, © 1984, London.

45. Josquin, *El grillo*. Reprinted with permission from A. Smijers et. al., eds., Josquin, *Wereldlijke Werken* II/5, (Amsterdam: Vereniging voor Nederlandse Muziekgeschiedenis, 1968). English translation by Tinelot Wittermans, used by permission.

46. Claudin de Sermisy, *Tant que vivray*. Reprinted with permission of the American Institute of Musicology, Inc., Middleton, Wisc. from Gaston Allaire and Isabelle Cazeaux, eds., Claudin de Sermisy, *Collected Works*, vol. 4: *Chansons*, (Neuhausen-Stuttgart: American Institute of Musicology, Hänssler-Verlag, 1974). English translation by Lawrence Rosenwald, Anne Pierce Rogers Professor of English, Wellesley College, used by permission.

47. Jacob Arcadelt, *Il bianco e dolce cigno*. Reprinted with permission of the American Institute of Musicology, Inc., Middleton, Wisc. from Albert Seay, ed., *Jacobi Arcadelt Opera Omnia*, vol. 2 (Corpus mensurabilis musicae 31), © 1970 by Armen Carapetyan/ Hänssler-Verlag, Neuhausen-Stuttgart. English translation of text by Alfonso d'Avalos from *The European Musical Heritage, 800–1750* [compiled by] Sarah Fuller; consulting editor in music, Allan W. Schindler. 1/e. NY: Knopf, © 1987. By permission of The McGraw-Hill Companies.

48. Cipriano de Rore, *Da le belle contrade d'oriente*. English translation from *The European Musical Heritage, 800–1750* [compiled by] Sarah Fuller; consulting editor

in music, Allan W. Schindler. 1/e. NY: Knopf, © 1987. By permission of The McGraw-Hill Companies.

49. Maddalena Casulana, *Morir non può il mio cuore*, from her *Madrigals for Four Voices, Book 1*. Reprinted with permission from Beatrice Pescerelli, *Madrigali di Maddalena Casulana* (Florence: Leo S. Olschki, 1979). English translation MEB.

50. Luca Marenzio, *Solo e pensoso*. English translation MEB.

51. Luzzasco Luzzaschi, *T'amo mia vita* from his *Madrigali a uno, due e tre soprani*. Reprinted with permission from Adriano Cavicchi, ed., *Monumenti di Musica Italiana*, Ser. II, vol. 2ed. (Brescia: L'Organo; Kassel: Bärenreiter, 1965). English translation from *Women Composers: Music Through the Ages* edited by Martha F. Schleifer and Sylvia Glickman, G.K. Hall, © 1996 G.K. Hall. Reprinted by permission of The Gale Group.

52. Orlande de Lassus, *Matona mia cara* from his *Libro de villanelle, Moresche et altre canozoni a 4, 5, 6 & 8 voci*. Reprinted by permission of Bernard Thomas, ed. (Bradford, U.K.: London Pro Musica Edition).

53. Isaac, *Innsbruck, ich muss dich lassen*. Reprinted from Kurt Gudewill and Hinrich Siuts, eds., Georg Forster, *Frische teutsche Liedlein* (1539), Das Erbe Deutscher Musik, vol. 20 (Wolfenbüttel: Möseler Verlag, 1964). English translation from *Norton Anthology of Western Music*, Vol. 1, edited by Claude V. Palisca. Translators: N. Greenberg and P. Maynard.

54. Ludwig Senfl, *Zwischen Berg und tiefem Tal*. English translation MEB.

55. Hans Sachs, *Silberweise, Salve ich grus dich*. Reprinted from *Jahrbuch für Liturgik und Hymnologie*, vol. 21 (Kassel: Johannes Stauda Verlag, 1977), by permission of Lutherisches Verlagshaus Hannover. English translation prepared for A-R Editions, Inc., by Salvatore Calomino. Copyright 2003.

56. Luis Milán, *Al amor quiero vencer*, from his *El Maestro*. Reprinted with permission from Charles Jacobs, ed., Luis de Milán, *El Maestro* (University Park: Pennsylvania State University Press, 1971). Copyright 1971 by The Pennsylvania State University Press. English translation by Nicki Kennedy from *Music for Philip of Spain and his four wives*, Signum Records Ltd., 1998.

57. Thomas Morley, *Now is the Month of Maying*. Reprinted from Bernard Thomas, ed., Thomas Morley, *Balletts* (1595): Selection II (Bradford, U.K.: London Pro Musica Edition, 1986), by permission of Bernard Thomas.

58. John Dowland, *Come, Heavy Sleep*. Reprinted with permission of the publisher from David Greer, ed., John Dowland, *Ayres for Four Voices*, Musica Britannica, vol. 6 (London: Stainer and Bell, 2000). © 2000 by the Musica Britannica Trust and Stainer & Bell Ltd., London, England.

59. Johann Walter, *Ein feste Burg ist unser Gott* (published 1551 in the *Geistliches Gesangbüchlein*, Wittenberg). Reprinted with permission from Otto Schröder, ed., Johann Walter, *Sämtliche Werke*, vol. 1, ed. (Kassel: Bärenreiter, 1953).

60. Thomas Tallis, *Verily, verily I say unto You*. Reprinted with permission of G. Schirmer, Inc. (ASCAP) from Peter Phillips., ed., *Renaissance Masters: English Anthems*. Copyright © 1995 Novello & Company Limited. International Copyright Secured. All Rights Reserved.

61. William Byrd, S*ing Joyfully unto God*. Reprinted with permission of the publisher from Craig Monson, ed., *The Byrd Edition*, vol. 11: *The English Anthems* (London: Stainer and Bell, 1983). © 1983 Stainer & Bell Ltd., London, England.

62. Giovanni Pierluigi da Palestrina, *Missa Papae Marcelli*, Credo.

63. Antonio de Cabezón, *Diferencias sobre el canto de la Dama le demanda*. Reprinted from Felipe Pedrell, ed., rev. Higino Anglés, Antonio de Cabezón, *Obras de música para tecla . . .* vol. 3, Monumentos de la Música Espanola, 29 (Barcelona: Consejo superior de invesitigaciones científicas, 1966).

64. Francesco Spinacino, Ricercar from his *Intabolatura de lauto*. Reprinted by permission of the publisher from Stanley Buetens, ed., *Lute Recercars by Dalza, Spinacino, Bossinensis, & Capirola* (Menlo Park, CA: Instrumenta Antiqua Publications, 1968).

65. Andrea Gabrieli, *Ricercar del duodecimo tuono*.

66. Jan Pieterszoon Sweelinck, *Fantasia chromatica*. Reprinted from Max Seiffert, ed., Jan Pieterszoon Sweelinck, *Werken*, deel 1: *Werken voor Orgel en Clavecimbel* (Amsterdam: G. Alsbach, 1943).

67. Tielman Susato, Dances from *Het derde musyck boexken*. Reprinted with permission of European American Music Distributors LLC, sole US and Canadian agent for Schott Musik International, from Nikolaus Delius, ed., Tielman Susato *Danserye*. © 1989 Schott Musik International. All rights reserved.

68. Michael Praetorius, Dances for *Terpsichore*. Reprinted from Günther Oberst, ed., Michael Praetorius, *Gesamtausgabe der musikalischen Werke*, vol. 15: *Terpsichore* (Wolfenbüttel-Berlin: Georg Kallmeyer, 1929).

69. Lassus, Prologue to *Prophetiae Sibyllarum*. Reprinted from Joachim Terstappen, ed., Orlando Lasso, *Prophetiae Sibyllarum* (Wolfenbüttel: Möseler Verlag, 1937). English translation by Thomas Binkley from *The Sibylline Prophecies: Prophetiae Sibyllarum; The Penitential Psalms*. Bloomington, IN: *Focus*, © 1985, 842 Focus. Reprinted by permission of Raglind Binkley.

70. Lassus, *Cum essem parvulus*. Reprinted from Allan W. Atlas, ed., *Anthology of Renaissance Music* (NY: Norton, 1998).

71. Giacopo Peri, "Dunque fra torbide onde," from *Il Canto d'Arione*. Reprinted from D. P. Walker, ed., *Musique des intermèdes de "La Pellegrina"* (Paris: Editions du Centre National de la Recherche Scientifique, 1963). English Translation by Cecile Stratta. © 1998 Sony Classical a division of Sony Music Entertainment Inc. Used by Permission. All rights reserved.

72. Giulio Caccini, *Sfogava con le stelle*. Reprinted with permission of the publisher from H. Wiley Hitchcock, ed., *Giulio Caccini, Le nuove musiche*, Recent Researches in the Music of the Baroque Era, vol. 9 (Madison, WI: A-R Editions, Inc., 1970).

73. Giulio Caccini, *Al fonte, al prato* from *Nuove musiche e nuova maniera di scriverle*. Reprinted with permission of the publisher from H. Wiley Hitchcock, ed., *Giulio Caccini, Nuove musiche e nuova maniera di scriverle* (1614), Recent Researches in the Music of the Baroque Era, vol. 27 (Madison, WI: A-R Editions, Inc., 1978).

74. Monteverdi, *Cruda Amarilli*. English translation MEB.

75. Claudio Monteverdi, *T'amo mia vita*, from his Madrigals, Book Five. Edited and Translated by Lynn George. Copyright © 1968 (Renewed) by G. Schirmer, Inc. (ASCAP). International Copyright Secured. All Rights Reserved. Reprinted with permission. English translation from *Women Composers: Music Through the Ages* edited by Martha F. Schleifer and Sylvia Glickman, G. K. Hall, © 1996 G.K. Hall. Reprinted by permission of The Gale Group.

76. Claudio Monteverdi, *Zefiro torna*. Reprinted by permission of European American Music Distributors LLC, sole US and Canadian agent for Universal Edition, from G. F. Malipiero, ed., Claudio Monteverdi, *Tutte le opere*, vol. 9. © 1929 by Universal Edition. © renewed. All rights reserved.

77. Francesca Caccini, *Lasciatemi qui solo*. Modern edition and English translation © Suzanne G. Cusick. Used by permission.

78. Barbara Strozzi, *Tradimento!* English translation by Carol Plantamura © 1985, Leonarda Productions, Inc. http://www.leonarda.com.

79. Étienne Moulinié), *Enfin la beauté que j'adore*. Reprinted by courtesy of the publisher from Andrée Verchaly, ed., *Airs de duor pour voix et luth (1603–1643)* (Paris: Publications de la Société Française de Musicologie, 1989). English translation © Ellen Hargis.

80. Monteverdi, *Orfeo: Favola in Musica*, excerpt from Act II. Reprinted by permission of European American Music Distributors, sole U.S. and Canadian agent for Universal Edition A. G., Vienna, from G. F. Malipiero, ed., Claudio Monteverdi, *Tutte le opere* (Vienna: Universal Edition © 1926–1942). All rights reserved. English translation by Robert Stuart, Chester © 1923, J. & W. Chester Ltd. By permission of G. Schirmer, Inc. & Associated Music Publishers, Inc., A Division of Music Sales Corporation.

81. Monteverdi, *L'incoronazione di Poppea*, Act I, excerpt. Libretto by Giovanni Busenello. Reprinted with permission of G. Schirmer, Inc. (ASCAP) from Alan Curtis, ed., Claudio Monteverdi, *L'incoronazione di Poppea*. Copyright © 1989 Novello & Company Limited. International Copyright Secured. All Rights Reserved.

82. Heinrich Schütz, *Singet dem Herren ein neues Lied*. Reprinted with permission of the publisher from Werner Bittinger, ed., Heinrich Schütz, *Neue Ausgabe sämtlicher Werke*, Bd. 15 (Kassel: Bärenreiter, 1964). English translation from *Dedication Service for St. Gertrude's Chapel, Hamburg*, 1607, edited by Frederick K. Gable, Recent Researches in the Music of the Baroque Era, vol. 91 (Madison, WI: A-R Editions, Inc. 1998).

83. Schütz, *Saul, was verfolgst du mich?* SWV 415. Reprinted with permission of Carus-Verlag Stuttgart GmbH, Sielminger Str. 51, D-70771 Leinfelden-Echterdingen, Germany; from *Stuttgarter Schützausgabe*, ed. G. Graulich, English text by Derek McCulloch. © 1969 by Hänssler Verlag, Neuhausen-Stuttgart.

84. Jean-Baptiste Lully, *Armide*, Overture and Act II, Scene 5.

85. George Frideric Handel, *Giulio Cesare* (excerpt). English translation © Harmonia Mundi S.A.

86. Henry Purcell, *Dido and Aeneas*, Act I (excerpt).

87. John Christopher Pepusch, *The Beggar's Opera*, excerpts. Reprinted by permission of the publisher from Jeremy Barlow, ed. and arr., *The Music of John Gay's The Beggar's Opera*. © Oxford University Press 1990. All rights reserved.

88. Giacomo Carissimi, *Jephte*. Reprinted with permission of G. Schirmer, Inc. (ASCAP) from edition by Janet Beat. Copyright © 1974 Novello & Company Limited. International Copyright Secured. All Rights Reserved.

89. Handel, *Zadok the Priest*.

90. Johann Sebastian Bach, *Jesu, der du meine Seele*, BWV 78, excerpts. Reprinted with permission of the publisher from Neue Bach Ausgabe © 1953 Bärenreiter-Verlag. English translation MEB.

91. Arcangelo Corelli, Concerto grosso in F Major, Op. 6, No. 2.

92. Antonio Vivaldi, Concerto in A minor, Op. 3, no. 8, first movement. Copyright 1965, by G. Ricordi & C. Editori, Milano. All rights reserved. Reprinted by permission.

93. Elisabeth Jacquet de la Guerre, *Pièces de clavecin*, Courante and Gigue.

94. Johann Kuhnau, *Musicalische Vorstellung einiger Biblische Historien*, excerpt from sonata 1.

95. Jean-Féry Rebel, *Les élémens*, first movement ("Le cahos"). Reprinted with permission from edition by Catherine Cessace (Paris: Éditions Salabert, 1993).

96. Girolamo Frescobaldi, *Il Secondo Libro di Toccate*, *Toccata nona*. Reprinted with permission of the publisher from Etienne Darbellay, ed., Girolamo Frescobaldi, *Opere complete*, vol. 3: *Il secondo libro di Toccate* (Milan: Edizioni Suvini Zerboni, 1979).

97. Dietrich Buxtehude, Praeludium in G minor, BuxWV 149.

98. J.S. Bach, *The Well-Tempered Clavier*, Book I, excerpts.

99. Johann Pachelbel, Chorale prelude on the *Magnificat peregrini toni*.

100. J. S. Bach, Chorale prelude on *Meine Seele erhebt den Herren*, BWV 645, from *Sechs Choräle von verschiedener Art* (the "Schübler" chorales).

101. J. S. Bach, *Aria mit Veränderungen* ("Goldberg" Variations), Aria and variations 1–7.

12

O.L. 202

10. Rose, liz, printemps

ROSE, LIZ, PRINTEMPS, VERDURE

A Rose, liz, printemps, verdure,
Fleur, baume et tres douce odour,
B Belle, passés en douçour,

a Et tous les biens de Nature
Avez, dont je vous aour.

A Rose, liz, printemps, verdure,
Fleur, baume et tres douce odour.

a Et quant toute creature
Seurmonte vostre valour,
b Bien puis dire et par honnour:

A Rose, liz, printemps, verdure,
Fleur, baume et tres douce odour,
B Belle, passés en douçour.

Rose, lily, springtime, greenery,
flowers, balm and most sweet perfume,
fair one, you surpass in sweetness,

and you have all the good gifts of Nature,
which is why I adore you.

Rose, lily, springtime, greenery,
flowers, balm and most sweet perfume.

And since your sweet virtue
surpasses every living creature,
I may well say, and honourably:

Rose, lily, springtime, greenery,
flowers, balm and most sweet perfume,
fair one, you surpass in sweetness.

Adieu ces bon vins de Lannoys

A Adieu ces bons vins de Lannoys,
Adieu dames, adieu borgois,
Adieu celle que tant amoye,
B Adieu toute playssante joye,
Adieu tous compaignons galois.

a Je m'en vois tout arquant des nois,
Car je ne truis feves ne pois,
Dont bien souvent [au cu] er m'ennoye.

A Adieu ces bons vins de Lannoys,
Adieu dames, adieu borgois,
Adieu celle que tant amoye.

a De moy serés par plusieurs fois
Regretés par dedans les bois,
Ou il n'y a sentier ne voye;
b Puis ne scaray que faire doye
Se je ne crie a haute vois:

A Adieu ces bons vins de Lannoys,
Adieu dames, adieu borgois,
Adieu celle que tant amoye,
B Adieu toute playssante joye,
Adieu tous compaignons galois.

Farewell to the fine wines of the Laonnais,
farewell ladies, farewell townsmen,
farewell to her I loved so much,
farewell to all joy and pleasure,
farewell all boon companions.

Off I go cracking nuts,
for I can find no beans or peas,
which often makes my heart grieve.

Farewell to the fine wines of the Laonnais,
farewell ladies, farewell townsmen,
farewell to her I loved so much.

I will often miss you
out in the woods
where there is no path or track;
I do not know what else to do
but cry aloud:

Farewell to the fine wines of the Laonnais,
farewell ladies, farewell townsmen,
farewell to her I loved so much,
farewell to all joy and pleasure,
farewell all boon companions.

Music 251
Paper #1
Due Friday, March 9th

Attached you will find scores of two rondeaux: *Rose, liz, printemps* by Guillaume de Machaut and *Adieu ces bon vins de Lannoys* by Guillaume Dufay. Write an essay (approx. 3 pages) comparing these songs. Use the following questions as a guide:

1) Describe the character and structure of the texted voices (shape of melodic lines, cadential goals, word/music relationships).

2) Describe features of any untexted passages used as introductions or codas.

3) Consider the functions of Tenor and Contratenor parts and their relationships. Discuss the relationship of texted voices and their Tenors. What functions do the alternate Contratenor (CT II) and Triplum serve in *Rose, liz, printemps*?

4) Describe the form of the compositions, citing features of the A and B sections which give them a distinctive character.

5) What differences do you find in Machaut's and Dufay's use of rhythm?

6) The Contratenor part in bars 28-33 of *Adieu ces bon vins* has not survived damage to the only manuscript source we have of the song. Do you agree with modern reconstructions of these bars heard on the recordings, or can you imagine an appropriate but different one? Hand in a copy of the Xeroxed score with the final six bars of the Contratenor part completed.

7) Comment on the performances of these works. Each of the songs is represented here by two performances (listed below).

RECORDINGS (on our webpage and on reserve at the Music Library circulation desk):

Rose, liz, printemps -- **(1)** Waverly Consort (<u>Record 7947</u>) **(2)** Gothic Voices (<u>CD 608</u>)

Adieu ces bon vins -- **(1)** Medieval Consort of London (<u>Record 17,436</u>) **(2)** Gothic Voices (<u>CD 609</u>)